WHAT I BELIEVE

22 Personal Essays

John Langan, Editor

What I Believe

22 Personal Essays

John Langan, Editor

Comments to any of the essayists in this collection will be forwarded and can be sent to **writersjj@gmail.com**.

To submit an essay for consideration in an expanded edition of *What I Believe*, request guidelines by writing to Townsend Press, 439 Kelley Drive, West Berlin, NJ 08091.

ISBN (print edition): 978-1-59194-801-8
ISBN (eBook edition): 979-8-35091-948-6

Contents

Preface

A college friend of mine who knew he was dying wrote his own obituary, declaring he had departed for what Shakespeare calls "the undiscovered country from whose bourne/No traveler returns."

The twenty-two essays in this book present personal responses to the reality that we must all depart one day for "the undiscovered country." The essays were written in response to the following prompt:

> Many people, especially as they become aware of their own mortality, adopt or form a belief system that helps them understand their purpose in the world. Write an essay describing your personal philosophy of life. The essay will be one that details the key influences and experiences that led to the development of your own special faith, values, or purpose in life.

The essays are as varied as the twenty-two writers included. For some essayists, a traditional belief system—Catholic, Protestant, Jewish, Buddhist—serves as a starting point for forming meaningful life values. For several others, an elemental humanism akin to the philosophy of the poet W.H. Auden, who declared, "We are here to help others," is at the heart of their belief system. One writer is playfully skeptical about a larger purpose in life, while another unabashedly celebrates atheism. A third finds meaning in pursuing the democratic ideals on which his country was founded.

For all their differences, each writer makes an honest attempt to arrive at an understanding of how best to live life here on this mysterious planet. Each writer declares, "Here is a life philosophy, a personal statement of belief, that has shaped and guided me."

PREFACE

What I Believe invites you to reflect on the diversity of experience in these twenty-two essays, perhaps prompting you to explore the convictions and values that guide your own life.

Dedication

This book is dedicated to two individuals. I thank my colleague Janet Goldstein for her superb editing and design skills and, more important, for her friendship over so many years. And I thank my wife, Judith Nadell, for being the sun that has warmed and illuminated every part of my life.

John Wood

John Wood has lived all over the world, including Chicago, New York, Seattle, Sydney, Hong Kong, and Beijing, and now calls San Diego home. He spent the earliest parts of his career globe-trotting with Microsoft, helping the company to expand its global markets. He left Microsoft to found Room to Read, widely considered as one the most effective education NGOs working throughout the developing world. In early 2022, he launched his second education start-up, U-Go, which focuses on helping young women in low-income countries to "shatter one more glass ceiling" by enabling them to pursue higher education with financial support and job placements. John is the author of three books, including the best-selling Leaving Microsoft to Change the World. *He was named by Goldman Sachs as one of the world's 100 most intriguing entrepreneurs and is a Henry Crown Fellow at the Aspen Institute. John is an avid outdoorsman, having run 17 marathons and hiked some of the world's most famous mountain ranges. He and his wife, Amy Powell, are active readers, wine drinkers, and global travelers.*

What I Believe

As a young boy growing up in a small town in rural Pennsylvania, I was always jealous of my mother on Sunday mornings. She had the pleasure of sleeping in, while I was forced by my father to wake up from my peaceful slumber, and told to hurry up with showering, scrubbing up, and putting on my Sunday best. "Wasn't Sunday supposed to be a day of rest?" I would wearily ask, knowing that I would not like the answer.

My mother enjoyed her lie-in for a simple reason—my father was as dedicated to attending church as she was to avoiding it. She was raised loosely Lutheran, while my father's family was fairly strict Catholic. He'd asked that they be been married in *his* church. This did not thrill her at all, but since organized religion meant more to him than to her, she let him have the win. She hated the prep sessions with the priests, finding them to be smug and sanctimonious. She wondered, "How am I supposed to have a man who has *never been married* give me all kinds of unasked-for advice? Who is he to tell me how to live my life and raise my children?"

She's a smart cookie, so when my father reminded her that a good Catholic upbringing required a regular dose of Sunday services, her response was, "Great idea. That can be the one day of the week that you wake up the kids and get them fed and dressed."

None of this was as rancorous as it might sound—just opportunistic on her part.

I often asked her, later in life, why she was not at least attending Lutheran services while we were at the Catholic church. She explained that there was just a lot about organized religion that she did not like. At my young age, I did not know what words like *sanctimony* and *hypocrisy* meant, so she explained them. She not only told me that many people in our small town would talk a good game in public every Sunday, and then be off cheating on their wives and deserting their children every other day of the week, but she also named names. I delighted in this secret intelligence.

She did not, she shared with me, need an intermediary to channel her communications with God. But apparently I *did* need that. I drew the short straw and was dragged off to St. Joseph's every Sunday morning, jealous of my mother and wondering how old I had to be before I could become a service-skipping Lutheran too.

There was certainly plenty of time to daydream; the long service bored me out of my skull. I was also really confused. What was the old white-haired man up front mumbling about while simultaneously dumping ashes on the floor? Who was St. Paul, who were the Ephesians, and why did they write so damn many letters to each other? How was it that we were eating the body of Christ *(gross!)* and drinking his blood (*ditto*)?

None of this was ever actually explained to my siblings or me. We were simply waltzed into church and told to sit down, be quiet, and not act up.

I could not wait for it to be over. I relentlessly tracked the time, via frequent and likely not-so-surreptitious glances at my trusty Timex. Every minute we had gotten through was one minute closer to the things that mattered on a Sunday, like playing kickball with my friends and watching NFL games.

The only highlight was the passing of the collection plate, but it might be more accurate to call it an ethical lowlight. My older brother Bruce taught me a neat trick. Every Sunday as we walked into the church, my father would hand us each a 50-cent piece to drop into the collection bucket that was placed on a long pole and waved in our face. Neither of us really cared about supporting the church, so Bruce instructed me to always place Dad's coin in the left pocket, while keeping a nickel of our own money in the right pocket. Guess which coin made it into the church's coffers? Suffice it to say the local candy store made more money from us than the priest did.

Almost as if to punish us for this financial subterfuge, next came the worst part. As the service closed, we were told to locate two people close to us and to shake their hands while intoning "Peace be with you." Never mind that we'd been totally ignoring these strangers for nearly an hour while sitting in close proximity. Now we were supposed to be bestowing them with some magical power (that came from who knows where?) to have peace in their lives, but doing this while trying at all costs to avoid eye contact.

Finally, the old guy up in the front spoke the magic words—"Mass has ended. Go in peace." This marked the first nanosecond of my Sunday morning that I'd actually been happy. Though once we got home, it was clear my mother—still lying in bed in a bathrobe and reading a book over her second cup of coffee—was in a jollier state than I was.

Some traditions fade. I think my father knew it was not working, as our attendance at church became more and more sporadic. He seemed to lose his enthusiasm for church—perhaps because it's not fun to force your three children to do something they clearly do not enjoy. By age 11, my Sundays were mostly spent water skiing in summer or snow skiing in winter. My mother and I would often hike with my beloved beagle Pretzel, as she told me that one can find God in Nature. No intermediary required.

With such an unpromising start to my spiritual upbringing, and with my fanatical devotion to books, science, math and logic, it might have been logical for me to follow the path to atheism. But for reasons that to this day I cannot explain, I believed in some higher power. I also wondered whether denial of God was too easy a cop-out.

As so often in my life, I sought answers in books. As soon as I was 2,000 miles west of Pennsylvania, on the campus of the University of Colorado in sunny Boulder, my exploration began. I read Desmond Tutu, Malcolm X, and Christopher Hitchens. I even tried reading the Bible, but found it to be ponderous and quit one quarter of the way through the Old Testament. I asked my friends what they believed, and why they believed it. One of my roommates responded by gifting me a copy of Sinclair Lewis's *Elmer Gantry* with a promise that "this will expose the hypocrisy of huckster preachers." As I studied astronomy and astrogeophysics my freshman year, I could not determine whether the vastness and complexity of the universe proved that God was irrelevant. Or that there was simply no way he *couldn't* exist, because how else could something this amazing be random?

At a certain point in my young life, I decided that I was too impatient for decades of navel-gazing and theorizing. What was instead required—no, *demanded*—was to search for examples of the actual implementation of religion, by real people. And then observe, connect the dots, and weigh up what the evidence told me. Pay no attention to words, but only to actions.

This might be a dog's breakfast of ecclesiastical memories, but here are some of the observations that became critical to my own personal belief system.

- Jesus is celebrated for washing the feet of beggars, but I did not observe many modern Christians taking extraordinary steps to aid the poor and the downtrodden. I tried to determine which religions were all about action, and which were just filling the air with sanctimonious words.

- What drove Martin Luther King Jr. and his followers? How can they be so screwed over by life's vicissitudes, but not lose their faith? How can I, who had won the lottery of life, not be working as hard as they did to fight for social justice?

- I could not understand why figures like Jerry Falwell and Pat Robertson seemed so mad all the time. They claim to believe in a loving God and in Jesus, yet they didn't seem to emulate him.

- The Jesuits, on the other hand, impressed me. Their relief work to help migrants was laudatory, and they had established hundreds of universities where students were encouraged to ask tough questions rather than blindly accept dogma. They encouraged a wide range of reading and seemed quite tolerant of those with different beliefs.

- It made no sense to me how so many religions denigrated women in so many ways. The priesthood was closed off as an option to half of humanity. Some denied young girls the opportunity to gain an education. Their message seemed to be that women existed to be mothers and wives—i.e., relegated to roles that preserved a male hierarchy.

The more I read, the more I decided that I would not give credence to people's words and would only pay attention to their actions. If a belief system was divisive, or taught their followers to despise people with different beliefs, those were teams I would not join.

❖ ❖ ❖

After I finished college, travel became a bit of a religion for me. Whether as a backpacker taking motorbikes and trains across Vietnam, or as a go-getting executive flying to business meetings in Dubai and Hong Kong, I could not get enough of the open road. And the more I traveled, the more I was able to experience belief systems in action.

I fondly recall the first time I experienced Ramadan in a Muslim country. It was a cold evening in Morocco's Atlas Mountains, and as the sun was setting, I felt a tug on my sleeve. A local man about 50 years old, bearded and bundled up against the winds that had etched deep lines in his face, motioned me toward the front door of his humble home. The setting of the sun signified the breaking of a 12-hour fast, and he was insistent I join his family in quiet celebration of the fulfillment of their religious duty.

Traveling through India, I learned to respect the quiet dignity of Sikhs, and the way religion requires them to give shelter and food to total strangers without any expectation of being repaid. Generosity was a belief system I could get behind.

During my two years as a soon-to-be-failed banker in Chicago, one of my high points was volunteering once a month to work night duty in a church that fed 40 homeless people every night, then rolled out cots and blankets so that they'd have a comfortable refuge against the winter cold. My friend Rich would sleep from 10 p.m. until 2 a.m., at which point he'd relieve me and I'd bag my four hours. During my quiet time alone, I'd ponder why some churches provided this blessing but why most did not.

An offer from Microsoft saved me from life as a banker and brought me to Seattle. Within a few months, a local shelter run by a Jesuit order recruited me to help stock the pantry before winter set in. I started a campaign amongst my coworkers, mainly of them flush with cash from the company's recent IPO, to throw down some coinage, and then spent a very happy Saturday with my friend Mary pushing a "food barge" through the local Costco.

On a business trip to New York, I was walking between meetings and made eye contact with a Pakistani taxi driver. He responded to my smile and head nod by placing his palms together and intoning *Tashabuk alsalama* ("Peace be with you"). That same expression that had seemed phony back in my youth now seemed genuine and alive with the spirit of brotherhood. Were these all random moments? Admittedly, yes. But what else in life do we have to go on? Isn't our life nothing more than several million impressions jammed together? If so, then the questions one asks are "What do I make of it? How do I pattern match? And then what, ultimately, do I believe?"

And then one day it all came together. Taking a break from the long hours and demanding pace of Microsoft, I headed off to Nepal to spend 18 days hiking the famous Annapurna Circuit. It would be nearly 200 miles of trails that would take me as high as 18,000 feet on the Tibet border, and I was euphoric. Each day's sojourn would be six to seven hours long, leaving the late afternoon and early evenings free for reading and journaling.

Though hiking alone, it turned out that I had the perfect travel companion. The Dalai Lama's *The Art of Happiness* was one of the books I'd eagerly stuffed in my backpack, and from the opening pages I was hooked. Here was a belief system that encouraged us to try to understand people who were different from us, and to ultimately love them. That taught us that the road to happiness did not lie in material things or great wealth, but in service to our fellow human beings. And to not stop there, but also to respect and give love to our animal friends.

These teachings came at a fortuitous time. On the second day of my trek, I had met the headmaster of a rural school, who invited me to take a quick tour. Like many schools in low-income countries, it was simultaneously hopeful and sad. Hopeful because over 300 students were showing up every day, eager to learn. Sad because of the conditions—dirt floors, no desks or chairs, and a "library" that was completely devoid of children's books. They had a few backpacker cast-offs, including thick novels by Danielle Steele and Umberto Eco, but nothing that would engage a young reader. I asked the headmaster how they could be missing something this basic. His answer seemed a bit like the topic sentence of poverty: "In Nepal, we are too poor to afford education. But until we have education, we shall always remain poor."

He then spoke a sentence that would forever change my life. "Perhaps, sir, you shall some day come back with books."

❖ ❖ ❖

During the next 16 days of trekking, I could not stop thinking about the headmaster, his adorable students in their bright blue school uniforms, and his request. I had promised him that I would one day return with hundreds of books. Expecting enthusiastic gratitude, I was thus shocked when one of the teachers shook his head, looked at me skeptically, and said, "Many of you trekkers tell us that you will help us. But we never see any of you again."

The gauntlet had been thrown down. And I picked it up, telling the small group of teachers, "I won't be that guy."

Reading the Dalai Lama each night felt like talking to an old friend who gave great advice. Helping those in need was the best way to live one's life. When we give things away, it does not make us poorer, but richer. If our main focus is on hoarding our own resources, then too much is never enough. A compassionate heart is a happy heart.

I toasted His Holiness with my dusty bottle of Carlsberg that had been carried into these mountains on a donkey track. In my journal, I reminded myself that the cost of all my trekking gear and plane ticket would be enough to buy several hundred children's books. And couldn't this be turned into a win-win? Since I had already fallen in love with trekking amongst these mountains, why not have an excuse to come back to the little village of Bahundanda?

❖ ❖ ❖

A year later, I did. My 73-year-old father, affectionately known as Woody, had helped me with a book drive and then asked to join me for the delivery trip. As a result, our six rented donkeys were laden not with Danish beer, but with books. It would turn out to be one of the happiest days of my life. There can be no feeling quite as inspiring as watching children who have never before seen brightly colored books as they literally stage-dived onto the books while they were still being unloaded from the donkeys. Their eyes were as big as pizzas and their smiles as wide as the Zambezi.

The only person happier than the students was me. At the relatively young age of 34, I had made more money than a small-town Pennsylvania boy could ever have expected. But I had questioned its meaning. I was bored while listening to coworkers talk about real estate prices. There was no desire on my part to buy a yacht, to check out of society, or to own several homes. Yes, I had success, but did my life have significance?

That day in Bahundanda, it did.

That night, talking to my father in front of a roaring fire over plates of egg-fried rice, we talked about what could be. Given that there were over 700 million illiterate people in the world, could we replicate this little library in Bahundanda a dozen times? A hundred? A thousand? I talked about other places I had traveled, like Cambodia and Vietnam, that also had great need. I believed in the adage "To whom much is given, much is expected," but would I dare to take on a radical implementation of it?

It turns out that I didn't. Until I did.

Life back at Microsoft was, as always, fast-paced and demanding. And lucrative. But after Bahundanda, it seemed empty. My heart was back in the Himalayas. I thought of the headmaster who had walked six hours round-trip from his rural village, simply to hand me a letter in which he requested books for his school. How soon could I go back? Every day his students did not have a library was a day we could never get back.

So one morning I reminded myself: "Look, dude, you've always said that it's not about words, it's about deeds." Within an hour, I nervously knocked on the door of my boss's office. Took a long sip of my coffee. "OK, you're not going to like what I have to say, so I am simply going to say it. This does not work for me any more. I need to quit."

On this day, my new life started. I was free from any obligation other than the one that mattered most—to serve those kids who had lost the lottery of life. Who, through no fault of their own, were born in the wrong place at the wrong time, and as a result might never gain an education. Changing this, and doing it as soon as possible, became my True North.

Did I leave a few million dollars on the table? Yes. Am I a happier person as a result of my decision? Most certainly. I may be financially poorer, but I am emotionally richer. My belief system drives my life, and when those two things are perfectly in sync, there's no limit to what one can accomplish.

Dawn Cogliser

Born in New Jersey, Dawn Cogliser grew up in a dysfunctional family and experienced a nomadic childhood, constantly moving from one place to another. In spite of difficult early years, as an adult Dawn was determined and focused. She graduated from Thomas Jefferson School of Nursing in Philadelphia and then worked as a nurse while continuing her education toward advanced practice. Along with her husband and their three children, she then relocated from the East Coast to Arizona, where they lived for several years on a reservation in the Navajo Nation. While there, Dawn again worked as a nurse and continued studying. After obtaining her master's degree in nursing, she passed the board exams and became a family nurse practitioner. Her nomadic lifestyle would come to an end with her family's final move to Oregon, where they now reside on their micro farm with plenty of farm animals. Dawn pursued additional education in the field of addiction medicine and now works in a rural community mental health center as an addiction specialist. Her work focuses on LGBTQIA+ individuals, and she provides care to what is often the community's most vulnerable population. When she is not working, she enjoys being outdoors in the beauty of the Pacific Northwest, where she can be found hiking, kayaking the rivers, gardening on her farm, or just relaxing in a hammock watching her farm animals.

Believe It or Not!

One of my favorite coffee mugs has the word "Believe" spelled across it in bright orange letters. Each morning when I get to work, I drink out of this inspirational mug. It's a great mug. It's pretty big, so it holds a lot. It has a strong, sturdy handle that fits my hand just right.

More than being the perfect container for my morning brew, the mug is a reminder of a topic dear to my heart. I'm someone who talks a lot about faith and the power of belief. I enjoy learning about the faith of others. People observing my actions (not to mention my mug) might assume that I have always had a strong connection to faith. They would be mistaken. In fact, my journey toward defining what I believe has been long and often rocky. It has been crowded with experiences that I am still gathering.

The journey began in my youth, which was filled with chaos and family dysfunction. I spent most of my early childhood in New Jersey in the custody of my paternal grandparents. They identified as Southern Baptist, with a loose connection to the church. They prayed before meals and when life circumstances dictated a need for prayer. But other than a cross on the wall and some Bibles from "back home," there were not many other signs of religious belief. Things were different when we went on trips "back home," which meant to Tennessee. Everyone in the family there was heavily into Southern Baptist culture. My Aunt Surry was the choir director and pianist in her small country church. She carried a small Bible with her everywhere she went. Her dresses came to below her knees, and she kept her long silver hair pulled back in a neat bun. She was a kind woman, and I always felt at peace around her. When we were in Tennessee, there were church events to attend on an almost daily basis.

During the periods I lived with my mother, I was exposed to various denominations, including Methodist, Catholic, and Lutheran.

The memories that are clearest are of when I was about 11. During that time, we attended a little Methodist church in a small town in Georgia. I remember that church fondly, not because of any doctrine I was taught, but because of the community among its members. There, I was able to form bonds with other kids my age.

While I valued those relationships, my experience in this house of worship was tainted by the dysfunction in our home. Those Sunday mornings always involved a rush to get to church on time. The hurrying would increase the ever-present tension in the house. Family members screamed at one another. My mother would often be crying. If I started yelling about what was going on, she was likely to smack me across the head. If my stepfather was around and I stepped out of line, as I often did, he would knock me to the ground. He rarely came along to church, and I was happy to leave him behind.

When we arrived at church, we were also expected to leave behind the reality of our lives. We had to smile and act as if everything was perfect. We were not permitted to say or do anything that let anyone know about the ugliness that preceded our arrival. As a result of this hypocrisy, I became furious. During quiet prayer times, I wanted to scream out loud about the lie my family was presenting. I wanted to yell out, "Does God know what is going on in our house?" Moments like these made me begin to wonder about the existence of God.

During the brief periods in my teens when I lived with my father and stepmother, I began thinking about atheism and agnosticism. As far as I know, my father was an atheist. My life experience was already making me question the existence of God. It didn't make sense to me that a supreme being would allow such suffering, especially for a child. My father's wife was from a Catholic family, and she took us to church and even sent me to religion classes. I don't remember a thing from those classes, except that I didn't like them. There was an overtone of rigidity that frustrated me to no end. The teachers were nuns, and I did not understand these women and how they lived. Later in life, I would end up working for a Catholic organization and became friends with many nuns. I learned to honor their journeys and the work they do. However, as a teen, being forced into Catholicism by a stepmother who I thought didn't care for me pushed me into a real rebellion phase.

Because of my rocky relationship with my parents, I spent a good amount of time living on the streets. I stayed in runaway shelters, slept in bus stations, camped in the woods, and did a lot of couch surfing. Even though sleeping in the woods left me exposed to the elements, those were the times I felt the strongest spiritual connection. Something about being alone with the forces of nature made me feel grounded, whole, and connected to a power greater than myself.

During one of these times in the woods, I met a girl about my age on a sandy beach deep in the pines. We hit it off and talked for hours. She invited me to her house, which she shared with her mom and grandmother. I was so impressed with their house. It wasn't fancy, but it was cool, natural, and earthy. They used branches for curtain rods, and beautiful rocks here and there for decoration.

The women informed me that they identified as witches. Here was an entire new layer to my growing confusion about faith and belief. They practiced their faith with a small group of other women that they referred to as their "grove." Their sessions together were held in a small, circular area in the woods behind their home. They referred to these gatherings as rituals. I attended several of them and observed nothing but love and kindness. I watched this daughter, mother, and grandmother conduct services that connected people and the earth. These women prayed in their own way to many deities, both male and female, although their primary focus was the Goddess. Their sanctuary was beautifully adorned with trees and wildflowers that changed with the seasons. I was intrigued by the emphasis on nature and the guideline of ensuring no harm to others. Still, as had happened with my exposure to other religions, I was bothered by the formality—by the rules and regulations that were invented by people. I was impressed by much of what these women taught me, although I do not follow their tradition. And I know that lacking a sense of family, I was drawn to these women's family bond.

❖ ❖ ❖

By the time I entered adulthood, I had little use for formal religion of any type. I felt bitter towards anyone who attempted to sell me on the "one true path." So I was surprised when a very close friend, who was also disillusioned by organized religion, invited me to what she promised was a "different" type of church—a Unitarian Universalist (UU) church. Intrigued, I went to the UU church with my husband. I was confused from the moment we pulled into the driveway. This house of worship seemed to be inclusive of many faiths—how could all this be under one roof?

The sign outside the church showed a chalice with a flame in it surrounded by symbols of various religions. These symbols included a Christian cross, a Star of David, a Yin Yang, an OM, and a Buddhist symbol. Similar signs of diversity were posted around the sanctuary. The church itself was a round structure built into the side of the hill. The building wasn't fancy, but it had a sense of warmth and inclusion. Greeters at the door smiled and shook my hand. The rows of seats inside the church curved towards each other, allowing people to look into one another's faces. But what I remember most was the people. There was such diversity! Some were in jeans and tie dye; others were in formal Sunday best. And there were children everywhere. I was struck by the way everyone seemed to accept everyone else. The children were not being ordered to be quiet; they were being embraced for being who they were.

As I read the order of service handed to me at the door, I noticed that this day's event was a "Coming of Age" service, which celebrated the teens in the church that were transitioning to adulthood. On the back of the pamphlet was a list of principles that guide the Unitarian Universalist Church. There were none of the rules and regulations or "you must believe this" statements that had so bothered me about other religious groups. Instead, the list included things like respecting the inherent worth and dignity of others. It went on to mention things such as the importance of social justice, peace, liberty, acceptance, and a free and responsible search for truth and meaning.

I was amazed as I read the list. I finally felt at home! No one was trying to convince me that there was one true path. There was respect and encouragement for people to open their minds and their hearts to the journey, both their own and that of others. There were Christians, Jews, Pagans, atheists, and more under one roof, all exploring this world of faith and belief. During the service, the teens stood up and talked about what it meant to them to be members of this community. I cried when a young African American woman, adopted by two Caucasians who were from Catholic and Jewish backgrounds, talked about coming out as gay and how the fellowship had held her with grace and acceptance.

For the first time in my life, in a place of spirituality, I was actually able to say, "YES! This is what I believe!" I had finally found a spiritual home, and I have been a Unitarian since that day. My husband and I have raised our three children as Unitarians and have never had a day of regret.

Being a Unitarian has allowed me the opportunity to explore with an open mind and an open heart, and to enjoy the journey. I no longer seek something that might or might not be. I accept that there are many paths and that there are powers greater than me. I can enjoy the exploration of others' paths and respect their truths while forming and honoring my own. This has been such a healing experience for me. As a Unitarian, I have had the opportunity not only to form a personal faith, but also to expand the facets of what faith should mean in my life. The Unitarian church is filled with beautiful families that might not be accepted in certain faiths.

There are families consisting of same-sex couples, interracial families, interfaith groups, and more. These people are a true representation of our world, rather than the fairytale ideal I was forced to pretend to accept as a child.

Now that I am happily rooted in my spiritual home, I have been able to welcome some tremendous adventures. For example, my family lived for two years on a Navajo reservation. We moved there because I was in graduate school studying to become an advanced practice nurse practitioner. Strengthened by our UU experience, my husband and children and I were able to enter into the life of the "rez" with open minds and hearts. Because of (I believe) our openness, we were honored by being allowed to take part in many traditional ceremonies based on the Navajo culture. I was able to befriend medicine men and women who took their time to educate me on their faith and share their practices with me.

My adult life has been filled with such encounters, some of them brief, but all of them meaningful. Each has added to the beautiful tapestry that is the blanket of faith I wrap around myself to this day. I have walked on mountaintops and talked with Tibetan Lamas. I have attended drum circles in celebration of Orisha. I have learned healing rituals from hoodoo practitioners, and I have held hands in prayer circles with Christian outreach workers ministering to the homeless. I have danced in the forest with Druids and celebrated the feast of the seven fishes with Catholics. I have attended weddings in ornate cathedrals, and, sitting on a dirt floor, I have celebrated the traditional Navajo wedding of a Navajo groom and his New York wife. I have prayed on my knees in front of an altar bedecked with three large Buddhas. I have held prayer sitting on a rock by a river under the moon. Each experience and each prayer has had one thing in common—gratitude for the life I have been given and the experiences that have filled it.

Looking back at my life's journey, I am so grateful that I have had experiences with people of diverse beliefs from all over this beautiful world. I have walked away richer from each conversation. I still giggle when someone asks me if I will pray with them because they assume I am of their religion. And I will pray with them. My prayer will most likely be to a different source, but the intent is the same. Every day, I pray for tolerance and understanding for myself, my family, and all those we encounter. As I learned that first day I walked into the Unitarian Universalist church, I pray that everyone will come to understand the importance of individual journeys and to respect the inherent worth of every person.

I am finally able to say that, yes, I am spiritually at peace. I have found comfort in the thought that for me, having belief does not mean that I identify a God. I am no longer bound by the need to fit into the mold of a particular religion. I am most at peace when I am living, and teaching my children to live, in harmony with the principles set forth in the Unitarian Universalist faith. This does not mean I pray to any set god or goddess. Neither does it mean that I deny their existence. It means that for today, I do not have to accept any manmade doctrine in order to "believe." I believe there is a power greater than I. On some days, that is the magnificent power of the elements of nature. On other days, it is the nurturing of the female divine, expressed as Mother Mary or Yemanja. And on some days, it is the more masculine, yet gentle, force of a Buddha.

I learn from others what they believe and how that fills them with peace. I do not need to convince them that my way is right. This acceptance of others only strengthens my faith. I am more whole at this point than I ever thought I would be. I am filled with certainty that my faith, like my life, will be constantly evolving. I am okay knowing that I do not need to define my spirituality. To know that there is an energy, a life force, and a power greater than me is enough.

This is my path to wholeness. And as my favorite coffee mug reminds me, in its bold orange print, the most important part is to simply "Believe."

George Mattmiller, Jr.

George Mattmiller was born in the hills above Puget Sound on the south side of Seattle, before Microsoft, Amazon, or Starbucks existed. As a teenager, he moved with his parents to Wheaton, Illinois, a western suburb of Chicago. Upon graduating college, George returned to Seattle to catch up with family and friends. But he lacked a game plan, motivation, and a general purpose in life. A series of temporary assignments and assorted odd jobs led him to the television field, where he finally found something that excited him. Over the next nearly four decades, he worked across the country in various capacities at broadcast markets big and small, from Anchorage to Philadelphia. In addition to managing and building TV stations, he wrote on-air promos, commercials, corporate capabilities videos, and two award-winning documentaries. But something was lacking. The biggest event in his life took place at a country church one balmy spring day on the East Coast, when God made His presence indelibly and unmistakably known during a funeral service. For the first time, George fully realized the imperativeness of one's eternal salvation and invited Jesus Christ into his life. Years later, while building a Christian TV station in Las Vegas, George wrote the novel The Last Soap Opera before Sunrise, *about one man's redemptive journey to a transformed life. George has participated in various street ministries and other faith-based activities, including Media Fellowship International, which serves the entertainment industry for Christ.*

How God Works

It took a funeral to wake me up. I thank God the memorial service wasn't for me. In retrospect, it had every right to be.

An adoring crowd gathered in the sunlit chapel on the manicured grounds of Pinion Acres retirement community. For years, Pinion had been a prominent advertiser on KWBB, the television station where I worked. We were now celebrating the life of Annabel Hopkins, the facility's *de facto* spokesperson, who lived to be a charismatic 102. Annabel had become an icon on Channel 36 because we used her in the closing shot of every Pinion Acres spot, cheerfully lifting a crystal water glass to the camera in a frail though heartfelt toast.

I fidgeted, wondering if this affair was ever going to end. As a rule, I didn't attend funerals. Why had they felt the need to schedule it in the middle of the day? Didn't they know people had to work? Then I realized that most of these people had stopped working during the Hoover administration. I scanned the room for Nadine Chatham, the Executive Director. My goal was to let her know I had a place in my heart for the elderly in hopes of continuing the station's lucrative advertising contract—but Nadine was nowhere to be found.

It was time for family and friends to offer tributes. Prospects for a quick end to this shindig were bright, as no one made a beeline for the podium. Then a big guy buttoned his suit coat as he walked stiffly to the lectern. This didn't look good.

"I'm gonna make this short and sweet." The rugged man stood 6'3", appeared about 50, and spoke with a husky drawl. "Some of us may have met before. My name is Willis Hopkins. You all knew my grandmother to varying degrees, but the common denominator is she loved you all dearly, each and every one of you. I learned a lot from Grams over the years, but nothing as important as building your relationship with God."

My heart sank. Here I thought we were getting off scot-free, and now he was dragging God into the picture.

"I think you'll all agree . . . none of us is walking out of this life alive." Leaning forward at the podium, Willis set his rock-hard jaw and scanned the crowd. "This is all going to happen to each and every one of us at some point. We're all going to die a physical death, and then it will come down to our relationship with God. That's the only thing we're taking with us from this earth. Do I have an amen?"

As some among the Pinion Acres faithful warbled "amen," I squirmed in my padded chair. This service had suddenly grown excruciatingly long to the point of being obnoxious, but Willis couldn't care less.

"If you died and went to meet the Lord this very instant, what would you have to say for yourself?" He gripped the edges of the podium. "Upon our physical death, we are all going to meet God, and we're all going to give an account of our lives. What will your account look like? Did you spend your life loving God and serving His people the way Christ taught? Or maybe you spent your life mocking Him and shaking your fist at Him. Or will you admit to avoiding and ignoring Him, taking Him for granted, saying Christ is fine for some, just not me?"

I broke into a cold sweat; everything started moving in slow motion. The dude bored a double-gauge reality check straight through me.

He was right, of course. I didn't have a thing to say to the God of the Universe, Maker of Heaven and Earth . . . Maker of *me.* I'd led my life the way I saw fit, taking God for granted when things were going good and railing at Him when things were headed south. I considered Him an impediment to my happiness, someone—or something—to just be gotten out of the way so I could go on living my life in conformance with my own homegrown desires and goals.

Willis Hopkins was strangely at peace. "John 3:16 states: 'For God so loved the world that He gave His one and only Son, that whoever believes in Him shall not perish but have eternal life.'" Then he nodded at me. "Physically, our bodies have an expiration date—but our souls don't. Your soul will live forever . . . and it will reside in the presence of God for eternity or apart from Him for eternity. Where do you stand on this most crucial aspect of your life?"

That did it! This guy had crossed the line. I would have wrenched myself from my seat and stormed out if it wouldn't have caused a scene. Plus some of these people were actually into it!

Willis Hopkins lowered the boom: "Who is Christ anyway? A worthy teacher? A fine man, a good role model? He is all of that to be sure, but most of all He is our Lord and Savior. God loves each of us—every man, women and child who ever lived—with a love we can't begin to comprehend. But he also despises our sinful nature. Jesus died on the cross, a divine sacrifice at the intersection of God's love of man and His hatred of sin, and through God's grace and mercy, we emerge as beneficiaries of this most selfless act in all history. Beneficiaries, if we accept what was done on our behalf."

It was a long drive home. I was doing a slow burn. This guy had torched me in ways I wasn't even aware of. In the ensuing weeks, I feverishly read and reread the Bible to discredit all this bunk and to show what an outdated instrument it was; those who subscribed to its wrongheaded tenets were, in my estimation, delusional dopes. The result was just the opposite. Over the next six months, the more I read, the more I yearned to know. I started attending a neighborhood church, hoping to trip up the pastor. Instead, I was asked to teach one of the adult education classes. I attended faith-based seminars and Biblical conferences, realizing I had more in common with professing Christians whom I'd just met than with secular friends I'd known for a lifetime.

While all of this was going on, my life was changing in myriad ways—some more perceptible than others. Movies, TV shows, and topics of conversation that had once excited me no longer held my interest. These pursuits were not inherently wrong or evil—they just no longer furthered my goals in life. I began praying that each day I would come closer to Christ, and to thank Him profusely and continually for what He did for me on the cross.

As I ultimately found out, once you accept Jesus into your life as Lord and Savior, everything changes. And if you humbly confess your sins and sincerely turn from them, all is forgiven.

I didn't think any of this was possible. But at the same time, I realized I didn't want to die without acknowledging my indebtedness to a loving Lord Jesus who went to the cross and died a terrible death for me. Since then, I have developed a simple yet powerful purpose in life: to live all the remainder of my days in focused preparation for that monumentally majestic, spectacular meeting with God Almighty, the God of the Universe, that will last for all eternity.

It took a lady 102 years of age to bring the most important thing in life to my attention.

And that's how God works.

In my industry, depending on whom you ask, it takes between seven and eighteen impressions to trigger the "buy" mechanism in response to a television commercial. In other words, people need to be exposed to your message, on average, that many times before they make a decision to purchase what you're selling. At the risk of sounding mercenary, the Gospel is really not that much different. I don't know how many tracts, street preachers, church services, and friends' testimonies I'd encountered before the Good News of the Gospel finally hit home at Annabel Hopkins' funeral on that fateful spring day in 1997.

I remember back in the 1980s working as a board operator at a television station in Anchorage, Alaska. We were airing a special for Billy Graham, and during an interview, the reporter asked Dr. Graham about Heaven. Without hesitation, the storied evangelist asserted that he was going to Heaven to be with the Lord once he died. What struck me was his utter, riveting confidence. There was no wavering, no backtracking. He didn't qualify his statement by saying "I don't know, I *hope* I go to Heaven . . . " No, he just flat-out announced he was going there. How could he be so sure? Wasn't that a bit presumptuous? It haunted me for the longest time.

Many years later, I traveled to Billy Graham's Crusade in Queens, New York. It was a sweltering weekend in late June. I attended both Saturday and Sunday services. Figuring it was Dr. Graham's last major event, I wasn't going to be denied. Even though I'd already given my life to Christ, I responded to altar calls both days. If there was ever a foretaste of Heaven, this was it. Billy Graham, the closest voice to God on Earth, led us forward in prayer while one of the headliners sang the seminal invitational hymn "Just As I Am." Moving in a sea of people on the wings of the Holy Spirit, it made the concept of eternal Paradise close enough to touch.

What happened to change my life so radically? It was a long and circuitous road, let me tell you. I was born into a loving Christian family in the USA, a country founded on Judeo-Christian values. Soon, though, the wheels came off; in what amounted to a dose of spiritual self-medication, I excused myself from Sunday school at the tender age of 10. I just didn't see how men in sandals strolling the desert a hundred million years ago related to me. Still, I had managed to retain the Christian brand throughout the decades and attended church religiously twice a year: Christmas Eve and Easter. So did that make me a Christian? Of course it did, through and through. What was I going to call myself, for crying out loud—a *Latter-Day Buddhist?*

During what amounted to my "dark-hearted period," the treatment I afforded God was nothing short of abhorrent. I was fond of boxing Him in, demeaning Him, questioning His existence, and mocking Him. Laughably, I considered myself more sophisticated than the Creator. At one point, I was writing screenplays in Hollywood featuring racy characters and chaotic plotlines that all but spit in the face of the Almighty. No matter; He was a little slow on the uptake anyway and would never be able to wrap His wrinkled head around my dazzling story arcs. I regularly went on an *"Angry God"* rant in which I proudly postulated that a loving God would *never* brutalize His Son on the cross in such a horrifically savage, barbaric way.

Oddly, when I was spouting these reckless, baseless assertions, I had no idea just how badly Jesus was torn up on the cross. It was much worse than I could have ever imagined. During the scourging session, His back, chest, buttocks and legs were ripped open by animalistic Roman soldiers who carved His flesh into ribbons during an absolutely ruinous display of carnal bloodlust. The depraved tormentors wielded sadistically customized cat-o'-nine-tails whose leather ends were fitted with shards of glass, metal and seashells to accentuate the "grab" factor. With blood spurting from severed arteries and bowels literally hanging out of His body, it was no wonder Jesus could barely make it up the Via Dolorosa, staggering beneath the weight of the 110-pound cross strapped to his lacerated shoulders. Consider if this had happened today: Jesus would be rushed to the nearest trauma center suffering from shock due to excessive blood loss. He would be placed in intensive care and receive microsurgical wound treatment, soft tissue repair, aggressive fluid replenishment, and massive blood transfusions. Even with all that, the threat of kidney failure and infection would make the chance for survival highly remote.

But Jesus's impassioned ordeal was just beginning. He was then nailed to the cross with tapered wrought iron spikes that were between five and seven inches in length. I have held nails that approximated the ones used to secure the Savior to the cross. They may not be as imposing as railroad spikes, but you still don't want them hammered through your flesh. Those administering the punishment weren't exactly skilled clinical technicians; they were bloodthirsty mongrels, intent on exacting as much pain as possible from their victim. It didn't matter if the hooligans crushed bone, severed arteries, sliced ligaments, and mangled nerves. When they finally managed to raise Jesus upright on the cross, the Earth's most regal and important inhabitant was reduced to a slab of bloody hamburger meat—and the worst was yet to come.

Death by crucifixion involves suffocation. You literally drown in your own bodily fluids that collect in the chest cavity. In some cases, crucifixion takes days. With Jesus it took but hours—accelerated by the shock of being totally separated from God. As Jesus bore the weight of the world's sins on His bloody back, His Father could no longer stand to watch. God's beloved Son had become a vassal of unthinkable iniquity. It was tantamount to dumping Michelangelo's *David* into a septic tank. Yet when all was said and done, the end result was the most selfless act of compassion in the history of mankind—and God did it for you and me.

This was anything but the "Angry God" syndrome. It was all about pure, unfiltered, undefiled, unabashed, unadulterated love: a love we can't begin to comprehend, define, measure, or understand. God loves us so much He sent His Son into this toxic mosh pit to stand between us and the screaming, highballing, inbound freight train of sin. We cannot even remotely decipher the dynamics that went into making this redemptive plan a reality. All we can do is say "thank you," realizing that God's heart was crushed in the unspeakable, supernatural process during which His Son became sin for us.

To this day, I still feel sorrow for all the insults and mockery I heaped on God during the years I strayed from Him. But the good part is, once I confessed these sins and repented of them, He forgave me for everything. The proverbial slate was wiped clean, and the relationship was—and is—allowed to grow infinitely stronger and deeper.

And that's how God works.

❖ ❖ ❖

In the rollicking bouillabaisse of yesteryear, I was intimate with women of all different persuasions, faiths and national origins. I actually thought I was doing God a favor by bringing the world closer together in a kind of a half-baked United Nations milieu. When I look back at the debauchery, the carousing, the arrogance and bold entitlement, I chide myself for lacking self-control. That's what's known as being convicted by the Holy Spirit. You'll find that the closer you get to God, the more these convictions sting. It tends to make you think twice next time before doing something that might end up being offensive to God.

Don't think for one minute I have it all dialed in and that I'm triumphantly gliding on a magic carpet toward the bejeweled gates of perfection. I'm still thumping along with patches on my tires and every so often—seemingly when I least expect it—I hit a pothole and suffer a blowout. But you know something? God understands. That's where grace and mercy enter the picture, the twin pillars of His undying, unconditional love for us. Grace and mercy represent virtues we don't deserve but are gifts God freely proffers. Eternal wrath, on the other hand, is a worthy punishment well suited to our sins—yet God refrains from meting out the thunderous pummeling due to one reason and one reason only: Jesus Christ.

The most seminal question in the whole of Creation—and spanning all eternity—comes down to this: do we have Jesus Christ in our lives? As much as God clearly, dearly, and purely loves us, He hates sin to an equally intense degree. There is no such thing as giving our soul a sponge bath—it needs to be power-washed with a pressurized frenzy that defies all human rationale. And there is only One who can administer it: Jesus Christ. By inviting Jesus into our lives, we clothe ourselves in His glorious regal splendor. By gratefully accepting the redemptive work He performed on the cross, we fully assume His identity. At the point of physical death, therefore, God sees Jesus when He gazes upon our souls; it is the radiant reflection of Christ that shields our otherwise unspeakably hideous, sin-riddled existences.

So really . . . who *is* Jesus? The children's hymn, released in the 1860s, says it all: "Jesus loves me, this I know, for the Bible tells me so . . ." He's your best friend, your big brother, the one who raced from His Father's right-hand side in Heaven to secure your rescue. That's right; He came for you and me to deliver us from the lethal hellhole we invariably create for ourselves—even if we don't give Him the time of day. *You don't need rescuing, you say?* Try this on for size: it's like you set the house afire and you can't put it out. You don't know how it happened, but you're sure it wasn't your fault. When the fire department shows up, you deny them access. The place is a mess—you would have cleaned up first if you thought you'd be having company. Does that sound familiar? Is that indicative of how things are between God and you as a general rule?

On the third day after dying that horrific death on the cross, Jesus ascended into Heaven to be restored to His Father. In so doing, He changed the course of civilization forever, exploding the shackles of sin and death that had imprisoned the entirety of mankind since Adam and Eve's fateful transgression in the Garden of Eden. No other religious leader in the history of this planet can claim they were resurrected from the dead. Moreover, what Jesus did on the cross paved the way for restoration of our right relationship with God. By proclaiming Jesus as Lord and Savior, people place their faith and trust in a loving, *living* God as personified by the impassioned work of His sacrificial Son on the cross.

To sum it all up, the original seed must first be interred before it can sprout to life as a towering tree. That's the whole point of what Jesus did for you and me.

And that's how God works.

❖ ❖ ❖

So . . . here we are: the end of the line. The train pulls into the station, and it's time to get off. If you've ventured this far without disembarking, maybe God is talking to you.

I'm not the kind of guy who goes running around ramming religion down people's throats. However, something did in fact happen to me that I feel compelled to share. Indeed, everything about me has radically changed since Jesus came into my life.

We were all created in God's image. It is said that each one of us has a hole in our soul that only God can fill. Sure, we try plugging it with all the usual suspects: booze, drugs, extravagant vacations, fancy cars, bank accounts, powerful job titles, impressive college degrees, trophy spouses, camera-ready children, and pedigreed pets. You know the drill. The list goes on and on. A relationship with God does not cost a dime, but we prefer pouring all these substitutes into our bodies and throwing all kinds of flimsy solutions at the problem when the answer all along is the One who started it all: God Almighty.

God loves everyone on Earth with a raw, haunting, exquisite power and gloriously desires each and every one of us to join Him in Heaven. Think of the vividly spectacular colors that await; the waterfalls of music and laughter of birds—we cannot even begin to remotely imagine the vast majestic horizon of hope sweeping across the infinite tapestry. However, if we deny God and reject Him out of hand, we're sending a message. And the end result will be eternal separation. Call it Hell if you want; it's the last thing God desires for us. But if we don't want anything to do with Him in this life, He'll give us precisely what we desire—even though it breaks His heart.

So it's your choice. You can embrace God your eternal Father, reconciled through the blood of Jesus Christ shed freely on the cross for you . . . or you can deny Him and live in a foggy anxiety about the final meeting between you and the Almighty. At the end of the line, after all is said and done, life as we know it will be finished, and our permanent address for all eternity will either be magnificently blooming—or tragically wilting. Which will it be for you?

The ball is in your court. And if this essay has started you thinking about your eternal salvation . . . then that's how God works!

Tanya Savory

Born in New York, Tanya Savory grew up mainly in South Carolina. After graduating with a degree in English from the University of South Carolina, she moved to San Francisco with vague plans to attend graduate school. Instead, she spent several years working various jobs—everything from dog groomer to bank teller—and became involved in the Bay Area music scene, honing her songwriting and guitar-playing skills. After spending a summer in Alaska working at a salmon cannery, Tanya decided to take a leap of faith and move to Nashville to pursue songwriting seriously. This materialized into three CDs and more than a decade of crisscrossing the country and playing in venues that ranged from nearly empty church basements to sold-out theaters. Finally, at 43, she returned to school and obtained a master's degree in English. Today, she lives with her wife and a continuing series of rescue cats in west Nashville and works as a writer. In her spare time, she enjoys birdwatching, stressful local politics, and running in the hills near her home to alleviate the stress.

Good Deeds and Joy

When I was a child, my brother and I often stayed at our grandparents' tiny apartment in Pennsylvania for a week or so during the summers. Prior to our arrival, my grandmother did everything she could think of to make sure our stay would be perfect. She put candy in little containers everywhere and bought cheap comic books for us. She made a huge jar of bubble mixture out of dish soap and created "magic bubble wands" out of old hangers. As I grew older, I came to realize that my grandparents were poor, though I would never have guessed it back then.

Every evening before bedtime, I'd sit out on the small front porch with my grandmother and blow soap bubbles. Sometimes the evening summer breeze would blow the bubbles back to us, and they would land on my cheek with a tiny pop. I'd screech with laughter, and my grandmother would sometimes say, "That's a whisper from Jesus."

"What's he whispering about?" I'd ask.

"Good deeds and joy."

I never really wondered why my grandmother said that; I just assumed she was right. I was six years old, and Jesus was a rather vague but nice spirit/person/being that supposedly looked out for me. When I read about Casper the Friendly Ghost in the cheap comic books, I thought Jesus must be something like that. A picture of Jesus (the one with his hair flowing and a gold light shining on him) hung in my grandmother's tiny kitchen. Another one hung over the bed where I slept. There was even a very small one on a stand next to the tub. That's weird to think about now, though it seemed rather comforting back then.

When my grandmother wasn't cooking or doing something for someone else, she read the Bible. My dad, her only child, said it was the only book she had ever read all the way through. And she had read it many times over. Grandmother lived by what she read. The Golden Rule wasn't just a pleasant thing to say; to my grandmother it was a serious rule that must be considered before all actions. Long before *What Would Jesus Do?* showed up on bumper stickers and T-shirts, my grandmother wondered about that daily, possibly hourly. And so, she loved, rejoiced, avoided judgment of others, gave everything she could, spoke thoughtfully and gently, and lived simply. She tried her best to follow the examples of Jesus. In other words, she was a Christian in the truest sense, brimming with those whispered good deeds and joy.

I never knew exactly why my dad decided to become a minister, but I'm sure it had a lot to do with his mother. He was very close to her, and he knew that his being a preacher would make her proud and happy—and it did. Perhaps he was moved and impressed by how much the Bible had shaped his mother's life in awesome ways. But did my dad become a minister because he was such a true believer? I don't think so. He doubted and questioned and struggled even as he preached and built a congregation. I know he prayed, but I think he wondered if his prayers were really heard. Even so, my brother and I were instructed to say prayers before going to sleep, and like most children, we were dutiful to God in much the same way we were dutiful about brushing our teeth. We did what we were told without questioning the deeper implications of brushing teeth—or praying.

When members of my dad's congregation burned a cross in our front yard after Dad preached a sermon about racial equality in 1966, he went from being doubtful to being disheartened. And when those same people began threatening my dad and then our family, he went from disheartened to angry. Who were these "Christians" who used their religion to hate and judge? Within two years, my dad quit the ministry. Our family went to a different church now and then, but now and then became less and less until it became never. By the time I was a teenager, religion was a murky and mostly ignored area of my life. Because my parents had become wary of overly religious people, I became wary too. Reconciling my new attitude with my very religious yet very wonderful grandmother was a complicated problem. So, like religion, I ignored it.

For many years, I mostly skimmed along on the very outer edges of religion. Church, faith, prayer—those were things for other people. This feeling was further reinforced by coming to terms with the fact that I was gay and discovering that many Christians wouldn't want me in their churches anyway. In their eyes, I was a sinner and headed straight to hell. By this time, my grandmother had died, but I wondered what she would have thought. Would this nonjudgmental and endlessly kind woman, with pictures of Jesus in nearly every room, turn her back on me too? The thought of it put me at even greater odds with "religious people." Eventually, I pretty much just shut the door to that room of thought altogether. I held onto a vague belief in God, though I wasn't really convinced that God might not like me. Religion faded into an unsettling nothingness.

Then my dad got cancer.

In his final months of life, my dad struggled quietly. He knew he was going to die, and all the doubts, questions, and conflicted feelings about his faith seemed to suddenly roll over him like tremendous waves. One evening, I walked into his hospital room, and he was reading the Bible. He put it down, looking almost apologetic.

"I just have questions, things unanswered. I wonder . . ." he said by way of an unneeded explanation.

Two weeks later, my dad died, and I was overwhelmed with things unanswered. I wondered: Was Dad in heaven? Does heaven even exist? Is he simply gone, returned to dust? Was God mad at Dad for losing his faith? What should I do? What would Jesus do? Who was Jesus anyway?

In the twenty years since my father died, I've reconciled how I *feel* about many of these questions, though I haven't definitively answered any of them. I guess I'm what you would call a questioning skeptic when it comes to my personal view of religion. It would be nice to think that all my grandparents and my dad are in "a better place," though the biblical definitions of how one is admitted to heaven are strange and troubling to me. The God I've come to accept is probably neither mad at my dad nor shaking his/her head at me, though I can't be absolutely positive about any of that. I have friends who assure me that I can be positive. But how do they *know*? Are they simply hoping that's true for the sake of their own eternity?

And what about Jesus? When I was ten years old, I merrily sang along to the hymns about Holy Ghosts and the Son of God, walking on water, and assorted miracles. But all of that seems a little sketchy and unfathomable to me now. It seems that many of us believe the Bible's story of the life of Jesus only because we've always been told we *had to* believe it, much in the same way that, as children, we're told we *have* to say please and thank you and behave ourselves. But religion isn't manners or rules. It's complicated and personal.

And, like my father, I'm often dismayed by the people who are the most vocally and in-your-face "Christian." These people seem to use their religion to judge, hate, and deny others, all the while presenting themselves as superior and saved because they are "believers." The great Indian leader Mahatma Gandhi once commented that so many Christians are so unlike Christ. Truly, it is hard to understand how some people who proudly announce that they center their faith around a man who was the essence of love, kindness, humility, and acceptance can be so totally the opposite of that essence.

Clearly, I'm not alone in the way I feel. Today, weekly church attendance is at an all-time low, and the number of Americans who identify themselves as Christian continues to decline. It is estimated that 60 percent of young people over the age of 16 will disconnect from their church. Naturally, there are the self-righteous churchgoers who shake their fingers and warn that this is a sign of moral decay in our country. I'm more inclined to think that it is a sign of more and more people questioning, wondering, and being disappointed with the experience of organized religion.

But beyond all the grey areas, disappointments, and questions, there is still a thread of comfort and certainty for me. It's a thread that winds all the way back to my grandmother so many years ago. I think of her knitting, always knitting, things for "the poor children" or speaking kindly to total strangers or being endlessly patient in all situations. (The time I decided to paint pictures on the walls with nail polish when I was 4 comes to mind.) When I consider that her character and heart were based upon what she read again and again about Jesus, it gives me faith in faith. It *is* real. It *can* work.

In my day-to-day life, I remain uncertain about *who* Jesus really was—the Holy Son who could make wine out of water or simply an amazing man whose love and words inspired people in incredible ways. But I am certain, thanks to my grandmother, that trying to follow what Jesus taught and said is a good thing. I have no doubt that my grandmother's faith made loving her neighbors as herself immensely easier for her than it is for me.

I'll never have a picture in my bathroom of Jesus or read the Bible twenty times. I may never feel comfortable calling myself a Christian. But I do have a sense of what's important in life for all of us, regardless of our varying degrees of faith and belief—*good deeds and joy.*

Tim Whitaker

Tim Whitaker is the founding executive director of Mighty Writers, a literacy program for kids based in Philadelphia. Whitaker began his career teaching fifth and sixth grade in Philadelphia before becoming a writer and editor. He was the editor of Philadelphia Weekly *(1994–2008), and previously the editor of* PhillySport *and* Pittsburgh *magazines. Whitaker was a head writer at NBC Radio and has written for PBS,* The New York Times, The Washington Post, *and* The Philadelphia Inquirer. *He was the executive producer of an award-winning audio documentary on the history of soul radio in Philadelphia and the author of the book* Crash: The Life and Times of Dick Allen.

What I Believe

Once a Catholic, the nuns would say, always a Catholic.

It's hard to argue. Catholicism, for me, and for so many, is as much a culture as a religion. If you're born and indoctrinated into it, there's no real shaking it. Catholicism may not be as culturally all-encompassing as, say, Judaism or Islam; but when you weigh its many dictates, its worldwide influence and its powerful Pontiff, it's real close.

Like all cultures, though, there is a great diversity of conviction among those who consider themselves part of Catholicism. Many American Catholics strictly adhere to the precepts; others, maybe more, pick and choose what suits them. And then there are those who tightly embrace the precepts in times of crisis only.

I began reexamining my own brand of complaisant Catholicism after reading an obituary in *The New York Times* for Mario Cuomo, the former governor of New York, who died on the first day of 2015. The obit writer referenced Cuomo's Catholicism several times, mentioning the governor's opposition to the death penalty, which the Church supports (though not as vigorously as the governor would have liked) and his backing of legalized abortion, which the Church most emphatically does *not* support.

The obituary included a Cuomo anecdote, one that will no doubt resonate with all Catholics, whatever their stripe: It seemed an engine on a Gulfstream jet had failed in a puff of smoke one morning—with the governor aboard. He barely noticed, continuing his conversation about national politics, until he spotted a reporter across the way. The reporter looked ashen.

"What's the matter?" Cuomo asked. "Aren't you in a state of grace?"

❖ ❖ ❖

When you're brought up Catholic in the late '50s and early '60s, as I was, under the supervision of a battalion of nuns, many prone to dishing out corporal punishment and humiliation in equal doses—all while insisting you affirm that your religion *and your religion alone* is the one true faith—you can either accept said doctrine with the requisite fervor and become a class favorite in the process, or rebel and be deemed a problem child.

By seventh grade I was a fully decorated lieutenant in the problem child sector of my classroom.

My mutiny against vigorous Catholicism began early and progressed in stages. Though the sequence of my uprisings is fuzzy all these decades later, let's just say my flouting of Catholic directives may have begun the night I devoured a hot dog at a big football game in clear violation of the no-meat-on-Friday decree. And then, for the sake of argument, let's say that when that trespass didn't bring on a flood of regrets, my disregard for the proscribed Catholic schoolboy regs of the era progressed to just maybe French-kissing Annie Leary under the football stands. I may have then conveniently forgotten to mention that delicious hot dog and my dalliance with Miss Leary to Father Burns during my traditional small-sin rundown at confession the next Saturday.

But my bravado had its limits. Within days I'd become uncomfortably aware that my youthful turpitudes had put me squarely in the Catholic red zone. I was traversing Earth with mortal sin. Those nuns! Which meant: If I were to meet an untimely end, I'd be damned to the fiery flames of hell. I'd spend all eternity with serial killers and Communists.

The following Saturday, anxious to get back to a state of grace, I came clean to Father Burns and was sternly told to say a rosary before leaving the church premises.

❖ ❖ ❖

The late '60s was a time of dissent and discord, as historians are always quick to say.

By now, the adolescent difficulties I had with Catholicism no longer seemed relevant. The vast majority of Church officials—the Pope, the bishops, the parish priests—had little or nothing to say on the moral issues that were dividing one generation from another: Vietnam, the draft, women's rights, Black Power. The Church, like so many institutions, didn't know how to cope with mass dissent, and so it stayed on the sideline, out of step, irrelevant, unworthy of even passing consideration.

During this time, most of the students at my college were from upper-middle-class Catholic backgrounds—the sons and daughters of doctors and lawyers and successful real estate developers, most of whom seemed content to maintain the status quo. Save for the occasional sociology classroom filled largely by a relatively small contingent of long-haired minor league rebels, there were few opportunities to process the issues of peace and justice swirling wildly beyond the carefully manicured college grounds.

I didn't recognize it at the time, but my connection to Catholicism was beginning to fuel a growing internal restlessness. A new empathy was awakening inside me that seemed rooted in the cultural Catholicism I had inherited from my father, whose own social views often clashed with strict Catholic orthodoxy, but who still insisted that Catholicism at its best was defined by service to the least among us.

I was beginning to hear that same point of view amplified by a new generation of freer-thinking nuns, and in the writings of Daniel and Philip Berrigan, activist Jesuit brothers who viewed their priestly responsibilities as working for peace. My interest in service to the less fortunate spiked when reading about Dorothy Day, a former nonbeliever, now a Catholic convert with unyielding passion for providing services for the poor in New York City. These were Catholics that represented the values I had unconsciously garnered at a young age and now as a college student. Their collective spirit was powering my desire to get outside myself, to reach higher ground.

Isolated, physically and spiritually, on a college campus where the sound of rolling beer kegs on Friday night had become the weekend soundtrack of my life, I wondered if I'd ever have the chance to put my newfound—dare I say it, spirituality—to the test.

In my junior year, on a whim, I registered for a theology class with the sanguine-sounding name "Faith and Relevance."

"We won't be dealing in the abstract here," Father Thomas Craven began the first day of class.

A powerfully built man in his late 40s, with rugged Irish good looks, Tom Craven had spent much of his priestly career working in prisons. He had been recently reassigned to a Hispanic parish in the city, 30 minutes away by car, but worlds away from where he now stood.

Looming large over us in class that first day, he told us he had been assigned to teach the "Faith and Relevance" class for one semester only. It was a directive ordered up by the diocese, he said, a dictate he didn't fully understand and was clearly not all that happy about. Now that he was here, stuck dealing with a class of largely uninterested college students, he seemed determined to at least do it his way. He assigned us only two readings: *The Grapes of Wrath* and *The Autobiography of Malcolm X.*

He ended that first class writing on the blackboard in jumbo letters the name and address of a volunteer program in need of tutors to help inner-city kids with their homework.

"Get out and see the real world," he said, turning back to face the class. "You might learn something."

The next day, I took a train, then a bus, to a forgotten neighborhood deep in the city. When I walked through the doors of the recreation center, Father Craven was waiting.

"What do you know," he said. "Somebody showed up."

He marched me over to a boy of 12 or so sitting at a desk working on his homework. "Darrell here could use some help," he said. "See what you can do."

In class the next week, Father Craven asked how many of us had made progress reading *The Autobiography of Malcolm X.*

Only a few hands went up.

"Your loss," he said dismissively.

He then talked of the transformation Malcolm X had gone through in prison. He told stories of the men he himself had met and counseled in prison. He'd seen men who seemed hopelessly broken reclaim their lives, some with the aid of prayer, others through reading and sheer force of will.

"Nowhere like a prison to see the power of God at work," he said.

And though I admired the power in his words, the mention of God made me feel anxious. It always did.

I had worked hard to avoid the do-you-believe-in-God late-night sessions that my college friends would fall into, seemingly as a rite of passage. The "God or no God" sessions would break out late at night, often fueled with the aid of alcohol, or something smokable, or both.

At my largely Irish college, everyone seemed to have their God answers at the ready. With few exceptions, they broke down in two ways: "Yes, of course there's God, how else did all this get here?" Or: "You're kidding, right? You really think there's a guy in the sky sending people to either heaven or hell?" Heady conversations, they weren't.

But the issue of God, and where he/she/it fit into my life, was something I couldn't address glibly or coherently—and maybe still can't.

Yet today, many decades from college, I can say unequivocally that, yes, I believe in God, and though I won't ever understand the decision-making, I have seen him/her/it up close and personal and felt a closeness. It took a while to get here.

When my much younger brother was forced to spend lengthy stays at a New York cancer hospital following a devastating diagnosis, I spent hours at St. Patrick's Cathedral between visits—neither praying, nor lighting candles—sitting in a back pew, alone, trying to deal with my sorrow. There, I found him/her/it and an uncommon God-like peace.

When my wife and I adopted a little girl in Mexico, we spent time every day at the town's Catholic church appealing for guidance in the silence. There, too, I felt the Presence.

And while living in Florida for a few years, I'd go to Mass in a church outside of town that doubled as a community center for the migrant community. The blessings I felt during those services came from being part of a community that embraced kindness and humility.

Did I find God in that church?

Yep, sure did.

Faith, for me, has always been a moving target. Separating faith from religion, religion from politics, has never come easy. Even now, as I write these words, I feel the rising of that old inner conflict: my desire to rebel against the convention of my religion versus the realization that its culture has provided me so much.

Maybe that's not such a bad thing. Faith without doubt seems, if not dangerous, a dreary alternative.

Back in college, with Father Craven providing real-world inspiration, I discovered a better side of myself. I worked with Darrell on his homework every Tuesday in that recreation center that semester, learning more from him then he learned from me. In class, after we'd read *The Grapes of Wrath*, Father Craven asked for us to join him at a local supermarket to protest the treatment of farmworkers. Later, he asked for volunteers to help serve parishioners lunch at his Hispanic city parish. I showed up each time. It was never an act of sacrifice; it made me feel good.

These days I head a writing program for city kids—not unlike the one that Father Craven sent me to all those years ago.

I am happiest when I am around these kids. In their triumphs, I gather strength.

At the end of the day, I rest pretty easy—content, for the moment at least, that I've found a state of grace I can live with, that makes me feel good. It's a state I've carved out for myself: light on theology, granted, yet aided by Catholicism, and, yes, the hovering presence of God.

Ayesha Rahman

Ayesha Rahman hails from Dhaka, Bangladesh. She spent her formative years in New York City, graduating from Hunter College with a degree in English literature and art history. Ayesha has worn many hats throughout her career journey and its many detours. She has worked as a TV show director, a scriptwriter for documentaries and short films, a copywriter for advertising and PR firms, and an editor and columnist for several magazines and newspapers. Ayesha currently resides in California with her husband and her two quirky daughters. She recently decided to switch gears and enter the fields of technical writing and management. When she is not writing about esoteric technology, such as mobile app development meanderings and humanoid robots, Ayesha can be found reading, writing for various blogs and magazines, cooking, doting on her daughters, looking out the window and marveling at the sprawling San Bernardino Mountains, or taking power naps.

My Personal Faith

Warm sunshine is seeping through the bamboo blinds and making fragmented patterns on the cold mosaic floor of our balcony. I can hear the neighborhood children shout as someone scores another goal. I desperately want to go out and play. My tiny feet are dangling from our smallest wicker patio chair with restless anticipation as I am waiting for the clock to hit 3:00 p.m. My *huzoor* (Arabic instructor), who seems exhausted, is sitting across from me, holding a cane, with his eyes half closed as I recite my Arabic alphabets. *Alif Ba Ta Sa Jim Ha Kha* (the Arabic letters) echo everywhere. My *huzoor's* head flops forward and his cane slips from his hand as he dozes on and off. Every five to ten minutes, he wakes up with a jerk and grips his cane more firmly. The clock seems to have stopped.

This was my first acquaintance with the religion of Islam. Needless to say, it wasn't a pleasant one.

In the early 1980s, almost every household in Bangladesh, where I lived, had a family *huzoor*. *Huzoor* is a title of respect that was given to an Arabic instructor. When I say instructor, I don't mean a licensed teacher or a scholar in Islam. A *huzoor* was merely a person educated in a local *Madrasa* (a specifically Islamic educational institution), and was a *Hafiz*, meaning he or she had the *Quran* memorized.

My memory of the countless *huzoors* I had over the course of my childhood is of their nasal monotones humming the *Quran* in Arabic, without ever explaining or translating the verses. And almost all of them stank and had bad breath. Muslim children back then were expected to learn the Arabic alphabet, learn to spell in Arabic, and then recite the *Quran* at least once in their lifetimes. And the stinky *huzoor* was there to make this mandatory task easier. Most of us did eventually reach the point where we could recite the *Quran* like a parrot. We recited it at least once in our lifetimes and then forgot all about it. We all knew what we had to do to get it over with, and we did, unquestioning.

Growing up, the only person I knew who was a devout Muslim in my family was my grandmother. I don't remember ever seeing her without her long string of crystal prayer beads. She prayed five times a day, and her house was like a shelter where people in need were allowed to stay for as long as they pleased. Cats too! She had stray cats and kittens loitering all around her house, licking milk from an unlimited free-refill bowl. That, I believe, is why I associated Allah or religion, and everything that comes with it, with old age and charity. I grew up believing Allah was sought in the loneliest of places and the neediest of hearts.

In my immediate family, the presence of Allah was palpable but never imposed. I don't recall my parents praying when I was growing up. I was never asked not to do something because it went against Islam. The kinds of clothes I chose to wear or the time I got back home at night were never called into question. My friends, my boyfriend, and my sister's string of boyfriends were not only welcome in our house but were also on great terms with my mother. Verses from the *Quran* were discussed over dinner the same way literature or art or science was.

Were my parents agnostics or, better yet, atheists? No, I wouldn't say so. We went to *Milads* (prayer meetings) hosted by family members regularly. My favorite part of the *Milad* was the sprinkling of cold rose water on a hot day. It had a calming, soothing effect. So did the pervading smell of incense. One of my mother's everyday rituals was turning on all the lights after the sun went down and lighting incense. She said it was to shun bad spirits. She also chanted "*Ya Salamu*" when I got sick—a verse from the *Quran* that is supposed to heal all kinds of ailments. She would hover over my head and say "Ya Salamu" a hundred times, and I would feel better almost instantly.

We also celebrated both Eids rather flamboyantly. The two Eids are the most important religious festivals in Islam. First comes *Eid-al-Fitr*—a holiday that celebrates the conclusion of the 29 or 30 days of dawn-to-sunset fasting during the month of Ramadan (the holy month of fasting). And at the end of the *Hajj* (annual pilgrimage to *Makkah*), Muslims throughout the world celebrate the other Muslim holiday, *Eid al-Adha* (the festival of sacrifice). During the celebration of this Eid, Muslims commemorate Abraham's trials and honor his willingness to sacrifice his son. They do so by slaughtering an animal such as a sheep, camel, cow, or goat. The meat from the sacrificed animal is usually divided into three parts. The family that pays for the sacrificial animal retains one third of the share; another third is given to friends, family, and neighbors; and the remaining third is given to the poor and needy.

I remember the slaughters on Eid mornings—the butcher with a special machete slashing the throat of the expensive cow or goat while reciting a prayer under his breath. I remember how the sacrificial beast would fall to the ground, squirming and then finally letting go with abject indifference. Then there was a communal meat distribution—not a soul in sight went home without a pack of meat.

And there was also collective blood—ripples of cascading blood flowed from the backyards or front porches of each and every household in the country. It flowed onto the streets and into the drains. A lot of scrubbing with bleach followed to get rid of the stench. I never flinched when the meat was served at the table. I hogged it all down. Sensitivity isn't encouraged in Third World countries. Emotions, social changes, psychological impacts, and traumas were not things one talked about back then in Bangladesh. I didn't know how to feel about the fallen cow early in the Eid mornings. But I remember the gush of blood made me silent. It gave me shivers.

Then a few years later, 9/11 happened. My mother and I were on a plane on our way to New York City when the two planes hit the Twin Towers. Our plane was diverted to Halifax, Nova Scotia, where we had to stay for four nights before we were allowed to enter New York City. Red and blue lights of police vans flashed and flickered, sniffer dogs ran to and fro, and policemen patrolled the airport of Halifax. We, the passengers, stood there in stunned rows without the slightest idea of what had happened and what was going to happen next.

That night we learned what really had happened and who the "terrorists" were, and I learned that the world would never be the same again. The TV news showed footage of the hijacked planes that carried out the attack. Clippings were also shown of the World Trade Center buildings; the magnificent structures were now reduced to ashes with all those thousands of souls perishing with them. At the same time, interviews were aired of people cursing and swearing at Muslims—now a synonym for "terrorists."

The grief that I felt then stemmed from twin tragedies: the loss of innocent lives in New York and the indictment of all Muslims in general. Hundreds of millions of Muslims had nothing to do with terrorism, and they grieved with the loved ones of innocent victims of the vicious attack. However, fingers were now pointed at Muslims all over the world. Hatred was everywhere I looked.

I failed to see justice in accusing and convicting all Muslims in the court of public opinion without the benefit of defense. The religion I thought I knew so well was one that did not condone violence and that believed in universal brotherhood, equality, and peace among all humankind. I could not comprehend how an apparent majority of Americans would define an entire religion as brutal, immoral, and unethical as the result of the horrific actions of a few individuals. The event of 9/11 made me realize how easy it was for a minority to become a scapegoat. I knew that no matter how hard I tried to blend in, I'd stand out because I was a Muslim.

And for too many Americans, I had become the "other"—the enemy.

Maybe it was because my mother and I both have distinct Pakistani features that give away our religion, or maybe it's because of our skin color, but that one-month stay in New York proved to be eye-opening. Family members constantly suggested that we stay indoors, friends considered changing their last names, and Muslim immigrants that we knew sorted out their life's savings to move to Canada.

My entire belief system, not just as a Muslim but as a human, was upended. I remember a drive back home from a family dinner in a restaurant when our car was chased by another car. Two twenty-something white males, one in the driver's seat and the other in the passenger's seat, were cursing us at the top of their lungs. I still remember the hatred in their eyes. They had their middle fingers sticking out of the windows as their car was zooming past ours in an attempt to block our way and stop us. A police siren made them take another route. But before they left us alone, they wished death upon us and asked us to leave "their home." We did leave after our month-long visit, but I was to return a few years later to attend college in New York City.

As a Muslim, as a woman, as an international student from a Third World country, I was in dire need of my individual identity. I attended seminars held by Muslim scholars, and I went to mosques to listen to *khutbahs* (public preaching in Islam). It seemed I was bent on proving something—proving to a vast majority that the act of a few Muslim individuals did not boil down to all of "us" being bad.

I knew that I loved New York City. I loved the energy it exuded. I indulged in the vigor and the life tumbling out of every street corner of the city. And I didn't want anybody to think badly of me, a Muslim, an international student from a poor country, loving the same things just as much as my non-Muslim local classmates. I wanted to be "them"—and yet also "me." I contemplated wearing the *hijab* (a head covering worn in public by some Muslim women) because I thought it was liberating and an in-your-face protest to all the discrimination and hostility that was going on against Muslims. But the illusion of freedom that I imagined would come from wearing a *hijab* was dispelled when I realized how the headscarf was considered in most Muslim communities. It was seen as the sole indicator of whether a Muslim woman was good or bad. A woman's absolute moral fabric was wrongly gauged by the fabric she chose to cover her head.

I wanted Islam to be the religion that accepted, forgave, included, and loved. But I realized that what it actually did was separate, ostracize, and scare. To start with, the forbidden list in Islam excluded the things I included the most in my life. My best friend from college was a lesbian. She introduced me to LGBT groups who were doing dynamic work in the fields of arts and literature. Being friends with her was like opening new doors—she took me to lesbian concerts and poetry readings that eventually got me interested in gender role studies. In turn, these studies later acquainted me with numerous writers and performers.

I majored in English literature, and my final thesis was on gender roles, which was part and parcel of embracing what was forbidden in Islam. I will always be thankful for the decision that I made at that time—to reject the religion of Islam then and there in my life. I also couldn't rid myself of my 200+ heavy metal playlist of songs because music was considered bad in Islam. I ate at McDonald's. I wasn't a teetotaler. The image of blood slithering down our front porch on Eid mornings still made me uncomfortable. I knew that there was still a lot of anger inside of me regarding the 9/11 New York City trip and the injustice of attacks on Muslims. But I also knew that reinforcing my Muslim roots was definitely not my answer.

My parents are devout Muslims now. My father has a beard and quotes the *Quran* as the word of God and not as a work of literature. My mother prays five times a day. They are old now. I do not understand their need to come close to Allah, but I do understand the need to have something to believe in when all four of your children and their children are in different parts of the world, and you aren't left with much. I can't picture myself in their shoes. Not yet.

I am not the kind of person a devout Muslim family would invite to dinner. I get frowned upon by Muslim family members for not praying, for baring my legs, and for plopping my daughter onto my husband's lap once every day so that I can renew myself in the bar in our family garage with a bottle of wine. I always close the blinds to hide the bar the minute a family member calls me on Skype. We have unholy images and objects strewn all over our house—images of naked women, Buddha statuettes, and posters of The Joker.

I don't recite the *Quran* to my daughter; I read Dr. Seuss to her instead. "One fish, two fish, red fish, blue fish, some are sad, some are glad, some are very very bad," is more relatable, I believe, than "In The name of Allah, the most Gracious, the most merciful Master of the day of Judgment." I don't mean to say that we don't teach our daughter right from wrong; we do teach her about the importance of love, compassion, empathy, and charity. We just don't feel the *Quran* is the right apparatus to get these messages across. There are more accessible books that teach important values and do not include the *Quran*'s fear of burning in hell.

My husband and I have countless debates over organic versus processed meat and health food stores versus regular grocery stores, but never once have we argued over *Halal* and *Haram* meat—meat that is permissible or not in Islam depending on how the animal is slaughtered. I am constantly reminded by my Muslim friends to say "*Mash Allah*," meaning "Allah has willed it," when boasting about my precocious daughter. I don't eat pork only because I am health-conscious, and I badly want a Toni Morrison quote tattooed on my right thigh.

My impression is that there is no such concept as a "non-practicing" Muslim in Islam. A Muslim is obliged to adhere to the teachings of Islam and perform all the obligatory duties. She/he must also avoid that which has been forbidden. There is no middle ground. I do not perform my Muslim duties, and neither do I plan to any time soon. Does that make me an atheist or an infidel? Perhaps. Islam hasn't proven to me anything of spiritual value in my life. To me, it is something I inherited from my parents, as they did from theirs. I do not, in any way, believe in a higher power or life after death. I believe in this life and I believe in living it—on my own terms, in my own ways.

What is left of Islam in my life is my experience with it over the years. Now it is mostly a flurry of fuzzy but rich childhood memories and images. The images remain an integral part of who I am today. I find solace in their memory. The images of a sunny balcony and a restless little girl aching to go out and play, or the touch of cold rose water on my cheeks, still make me smile. Whenever we come across a mosque, I ask my daughter if she'd like to go inside the "dome buildings" so that we both can sit on the cold tile floor and wait for someone to sprinkle us with rose water. I am secretly glad that her answer is almost always No. I do not want her to share my history, my baggage. Yet when she is sick, I sometimes find myself hovering over her sleeping face and chanting "Ya Salamu" one hundred times.

I light incense occasionally and turn on all our lights after the sun goes down. I run my fingers along a string of crystal prayer beads on lonely nights and hope all my grandmother's prayers went answered. I think about my parents often, and I am grateful that they have found their Allah now that they need him the most. But on most days, I do all this while listening to heavy metal music and craving a Big Mac!

Dick Kratz

Dick Kratz grew up in Newtown, Bucks County, Pennsylvania. He was the son of educators but graduated from high school with a less than stellar record. After one year of college, he dropped out, lacking the discipline and maturity to be a successful student. He then worked for a year with Abbotts Dairy, and after a short return to college, he signed a professional contract with the Boston Red Sox and played for that organization for five years before deciding he was not good enough to play in the Majors. He married Barbara Johnson in 1966 and, with her, raised two boys, completed his college degree, and began a professional career that was to last 39 years—spent primarily at two community colleges. During that time, he earned a doctorate in Higher Education Leadership from the University of Pennsylvania and served for five years as president and president emeritus of Reading Area Community College.

What I Believe

As I grow older—I am 77 years of age—I become more and more convinced, at least to some extent, that there is an element of luck involved in many aspects of our lives. My life has been no exception to this conviction. I had the good fortune to be born to caring and loving parents who saw their role as parents as their most important responsibility in life.

I grew up in the 1940s and 1950s in a small town of, maybe, 1,500 inhabitants. At that time, in this town, there were certain expectations for individuals and families. One of those expectations was that you not only were a member of one of the churches, but that you attended on a fairly regular basis. My family belonged to the Presbyterian Church, and we did as expected and attended weekly, almost without fail. The only exception was the month of August, when many families would take a "pass" on church. But when I was in my formative years—let's say 8 to 12 years of age—although my parents may not have attended in August, I did. I felt a real need to be there, because this was where God expected me to be on Sunday morning. In the interest of transparency, I confess that I am not sure how much I bought into the belief of predestination that was common among Presbyterians. Still, at that point in my life, I took my faith very seriously, and I appreciate my parents' encouragement to do so.

As I moved into my high school years, my participation in church-related activities started to wane. This was due to the facts that, among my peers, going to church was not "cool," and that I was heavily involved in sports. In college, I was still playing sports year 'round, and it is safe to say that my faith went on a hiatus. But in my junior year, a girl that I had been dating and I began to get serious about our future. She was not only the nicest and prettiest girl that I had ever met, but she was also someone whom I wanted to spend my life with. She was someone with a very strong faith, and we would talk about this faith being the center of our family and home.

It became clear that as our love for one another continued to grow, so too did our Christian faith. We have been married for fifty-two years, and our church and Jesus Christ are at the center of our faith. We raised two sons who were active in church throughout their high school years. I wish that I could say that both are very active members of their church today, but this would not be true. However, my wife and I can say with great pride that both boys, now men, care very much about others, and they spend time helping those less fortunate.

But let me turn to the real purpose of this essay: what do I believe? When I think about this question, I am always reminded of the famous long-time Pittsburgh Pirates Hall of Fame baseball player, Wilver ("Willie") Stargell. On this particular day, Willie was being interviewed, and he was asked what he knew about life. Willie gave a very long answer, but he ended with "And I know that I know what I don't know." And for me, and what I believe, there is so much that I "know that I don't know" about my faith. Maybe the reality is that I don't have the aptitude that would allow me to understand what "I don't know." Dr. Eben Alexander, in his book *Proof of Heaven*, talks about our concept of time here on Earth as compared to time in heaven. There is not a 24-hour clock in heaven—time is not of the essence—and this is a difficult concept for me to grasp and understand. Maybe this explains my lack of ability to fully comprehend some of the issues that I have with my faith. Vickie Girard, in her book *There's No Place Like Hope: A Guide to Beating Cancer in Mind-Sized Bites*, was "spot on" when she wrote: "During the worst part of her battle with cancer, one of my dearest friends, a woman of limitless faith, said it best: 'God sure has a lot of explaining to do when I get there.'"

With this said, let me make it clear that I consider myself a person of faith. Clearly, like most, I believe, I have doubts about God, my faith, and more. But as Paul Tillich, the Protestant theologian, reminds us: "Doubt is not the opposite of faith, it is the element of faith." The Rev. Dr. Martin Luther King Jr. said, "Faith is taking the first step even when you don't see the whole staircase." I believe in God, and I believe that Jesus Christ was the Son of God. I believe that God created everything, and part of that order includes the theory of evolution. Dr. Francis S. Collins, who headed the Human Genome project, and who was an atheist prior to completion of this project, wrote *The Language of God* in 2006. One of his theories is that God created the universe and all of its inhabitants, but God does not interfere with our day-to-day activities on Earth. I share Collins's belief. God does, however, provide us with a roadmap as to how we should live our lives, as individuals and as communities. I believe that God does this through the Bible, prayer, and the church. I also believe that we each have an innate knowledge of right and wrong, sometimes called Moral Law.

I spent about 95% of my professional career working in two community colleges in different parts of Pennsylvania—the other 5% was spent teaching in elementary, junior high, and senior high schools. One community college had a large enrollment of approximately 10,000 students and was located in the eastern part of Pennsylvania. This college was situated on a bucolic 200-acre campus in a well-to-do county, and most students came from a mid-range of social-economic-standing (SES). The other community college was small with an enrollment of about 5,000 students, and was located in an inner city of approximately 75,000 residents in central Pennsylvania. The overwhelming majority of these students came from families whose SES was well below the mid-range. I worked at the larger community college for 18 years and at the smaller, inner-city college for 20 years. Both community colleges espoused the egalitarian purpose that is one of the hallmarks of community colleges. And I am often asked which of these two community colleges gave me my greatest satisfaction and rewards. I do not believe that this is a fair question because both experiences were very different in so many ways. But clearly, from a faith-based perspective, my work at the smaller, inner-city college provided me with tremendous professional and personal satisfaction. It is here where I believe that I had an opportunity to "walk the talk" of my faith through word and deed.

My faith tells me that I not only have to care about other people, but I also have to help them to help themselves. I subscribe to Benjamin Franklin's axiom that "God helps those who help themselves." The community college provides that vehicle for students to better their lot in life. It provides hope and opportunity. But in my opinion, many of these students are apprehensive about life in general and studying at a community college in particular. They are just "not sure" that they are cut out for college. One of my greatest joys was to speak with the incoming students, most of whom sat in front of me looking scared and absolutely certain that they would not graduate in two years. I felt a real need to encourage these students, to make certain that they knew that the faculty and staff would do all within their power to make certain that they were successful. This was our job. So I would begin with what I hoped were words of inspiration from Rene Portland, the legendary women's basketball coach at Penn State. Coach Portland said that to be successful in life, we need three bones: We need a "wish bone" because we all need dreams and aspirations; we need a "funny bone" because we all need the ability to laugh at ourselves; and finally, we need a "back bone" because we have to have the courage to pursue our goals and dreams. And then I would go on about not being afraid to fail—not that I encouraged failure, but it comes with our pursuit of dreams—and then I would enumerate a myriad of failures that I had to deal with throughout my life. And I would let them know that some of America's greatest leaders, Lincoln for example, endured some horrific defeats and tragedy in politics and in life. And then I would finish with the famous quote by John Greenleaf Whittier: "For all sad words of tongue and pen, the saddest are these: 'It might have been.'"

I often gauge a person's reaction to what I have said by observing their eyes. (Some say that the eyes are a direct link to a person's heart.) In person after person I could see these students start to feel better about their freshman year in college, and begin to realize that they could be successful. This was later confirmed by their comments to me when I handed them their diplomas at commencement exercises. This talk with incoming students at orientation, and subsequent conversations with them in the student union or elsewhere, was my way of exemplifying a caring attitude about others, which is a basic tenet of my faith.

I said earlier in this essay that I believed in God, but that I had some doubts about certain issues connected to my faith. For example, I do not believe that the Bible is inerrant, and I am not convinced that the Bible is exclusively the word of God. For me, there are too many inconsistencies and contradictions. Moreover, there are some issues that I just cannot accept. For example, Genesis 3:16 states that women are subjected to men. I think of my love, respect, and admiration for my wife, and there is just no way that either one of us would concur with this doctrine. And heaven is another concern. I sometimes believe that heaven is a man-made construct to provide hope for oppressed people and those at the margin. Heaven, after all, promises all believers a better life through eternity—and eternity is another concept that is difficult for me to grasp; after all, eternity is a very, very long time. But as the aforementioned book, *Proof of Heaven*, indicates, heaven is a totally different place from all experiences here on Earth. And there are other issues with my faith that cause me difficulty in understanding. The Holy Trinity, for example, is another concept that I have never understood despite many and extensive discussions with believers who totally subscribe to this concept.

And yet, although there are sections of the Bible that I cannot agree with, there are other parts that I completely agree with and try to emulate. For example, I Corinthians: 13:13 states that

"Meanwhile these three remain: faith, hope, and love; and the greatest of these is love." And for me, the Ten Commandments and the Beatitudes, both found in Jesus's Sermon on the Mount (Matthew 5–7), have special meaning. These words are not only inspirational, but they also tell us how to live our lives in a Christian manner.

Finally, I would like to discuss prayer and the power that it holds for me. I don't believe that God sits somewhere and hears our individual prayers. But at the same time, there is something in my prayers that works—although I cannot be sure how it works. I have never asked God to help me get a job or allow me to win at some competitive endeavor. What I do pray for, however, is for God to allow me to be the person that I am. For example, I can recall walking down a hallway for a potentially contentious meeting with one of the unions over contractual negotiations that were not going well, with a faculty strike looming on the horizon. I prayed to God—all while still walking down the hall—to let me be the person that I really am, and let me be ruthlessly honest, but not in a mean or antagonistic manner—so that there can be no misunderstanding of my position. There were other times that I would pray to God to let me do "the right thing." I always remember something Father Theodore Hesburgh, the late President of the University of Notre Dame, said in his book *God, Country, and Notre Dame:* "We don't do things because they are politically correct, and we don't do things to win friends and influence people; we do things because they are the right thing to do." Although I did not pray that often, in each instance, I would come away from prayer with a feeling of relaxation, that things would be fine, and that I knew what I had to do.

So "what do I believe?" I believe in God; I believe that I have a responsibility to do good for others; I believe that I must care about others, and especially those less fortunate than me. I believe that love is the greatest human quality that a person can possess, but it must be shared. I believe that God created everything in an evolutionary manner, and that God stays out of our day-to-day activities. Although I suspect that I will not live to see it, I look forward with great anticipation to Jesus's return to Earth—although I fear that He will be disappointed in what He finds. I believe in the beauty of small things like a walk in the woods, nature, and the seasons of the year. And finally, I believe in the beauty of the big things like the love you feel when your spouse and/or children return after an absence. This feeling of love is all-powerful. The Scriptures are right!

Janet Goldstein

Janet Goldstein, a native Philadelphian, has loved the written word since age 4, when her father sent her letters from his posting in the Philippine Islands during World War II. She realized she had writing ability when her ninth grade English teacher, after reading her first book report, accused her of having copied it from the book jacket because "no ninth-grader could have written this." Recovering from that false accusation, Janet went on to earn undergraduate and graduate degrees from Harvard and then, after getting married, spent 30 rewarding years as a high school English teacher. During this time, she coauthored a grammar book and published several poems in English Journal *and a series of brief vignettes about her cats in* Faith and Inspiration. *She left teaching when offered the opportunity to help millions of students by becoming the design and print editor for a start-up educational publishing company. When not immersed in editing and writing, Janet has enjoyed swimming, choral singing, travel, beading, birdwatching, reading and watching British mysteries, and rooting for her beloved Eagles (who* almost *won the Super Bowl in 2023) and Phillies (who* almost *won the World Series in 2022).*

Seeing the Light

My formative years basically did not contain religion. Religion, in the traditional sense, was simply not a part of my life.

I was born Jewish, as were my parents, but all three of us were nonpracticing, and I assume they were nonbelievers. My father, the youngest of nine children, had worked at three jobs to put himself through college and medical school. He and my mother, whom he met in college, waited nine years to marry—neither of them had any money. And then they waited another seven years to have a child, reluctant to bring a new life into a world that also contained Adolf Hitler.

What my parents had, instead of religion, was a set of ethical principles by which they lived and which they exemplified. They believed in the values of hard work and education. They appreciated culture, especially theater; and they took me to many plays, even when I was too young to understand them. And they cared for others, believing strongly in "giving back." My mother, a social worker before she married, became a homemaker, caring for us while also volunteering at a local hospital. My father, now a 37-year-old physician with a wife, a one-year-old daughter, and a growing private practice, left all of these behind to serve his country in World War II. He joined the U.S. Army Medical Corps, eventually becoming commanding officer of a station hospital in the South Pacific.

As their child, I simply took my parents' principles for granted. This is how we lived. Religion had nothing to do with it, or with us.

After Dad was discharged in 1946, he bought a home in center city Philadelphia, on Spruce Street—"doctors' row"—and set up his office on the first floor, so we lived "over the store." Two blocks away was a synagogue, Beth Zion. My parents were not members, but I was permitted to attend its Sunday school, aka

Hebrew school. I went to Hebrew school not for religious reasons, but because my friends did. Hebrew school made me feel special in some ways; I became more aware of my Jewish heritage and enjoyed learning more about it. But I was still not a believer.

Then in the fall of 1955, the beginning of my junior year in high school, I was enrolled in the confirmation class. My parents joined the synagogue that year, only because membership was a prerequisite for confirmation. Members of the class were required to attend a certain number of Friday night services, accompanied by their parents. In addition, I was chosen to chant the *Haftorah,* a weekly selection from the Hebrew Bible, traditionally assigned, back then, to a boy. However, my confirmation class consisted of four girls. Even at age 15, I had a pleasant singing voice and had sung in the school choir and the annual musicals for years, so the honor fell to me.

I was terrified—no way could I stand up and chant before the entire congregation, *all by myself!*—but I eventually accepted the challenge of learning to perform the several pages of Hebrew. After the ceremony, I was told that I had done quite well. I was proud of myself (and more than a little relieved). But I didn't believe that the *Haftorah* I had chanted had anything to do with me, personally. Nor did the confirmation ceremony—despite the fact that I wanted to be part of it—make me feel any different afterward.

To be honest, what spoke to me more than Judaism was Quakerism. Quakers, also known as the Society of Friends, believe that all people have access to the Inner Light, a direct awareness of and communication with God. This core belief explains why

— Quakers respect the uniqueness of individuals because "there is that of God in everyone";

— Quakers do not have clergy to lead their services, since they do not require a "middleperson" to interpret the Word of God;

— in a Quaker wedding, the couple—once they "render unto Caesar" by obtaining a marriage license—marry themselves.

Quakers work for the good of others. They value simplicity: "Live simply so that others may simply live." They are pacifists. And they honor the power of silence. For these reasons, Quakerism has been described as "a way of life, rather than a set of beliefs."

I discovered this way of life as a sixth-grader, newly admitted to Friends Select School, a Quaker school within walking distance of my Spruce Street home. (Thirteen years after graduation, I would return there as head of the English Department.) Besides the usual classes, students and teachers were required to attend weekly Meeting for Worship, a silent service during which any of us could rise and speak, if we felt moved to—theoretically inspired by "that of God within us." We also had to take a course, "Religious Thought," essentially Bible study: in ninth grade, my class read the Old Testament in the fall and the New Testament in the spring. There were also service projects every year for every grade, such as packing donated clothing to be shipped overseas. Seniors had the privilege, for their service project, of washing teachers' cars!

All these things were positive experiences—activities that interrupted the usual daily lock-step schedule of classes and let me feel good about myself. But I didn't fully appreciate Quakerism back then. It was many years before I realized that its principles, along with my parents' example, had quietly shaped my life.

I filled a few of those years with college and graduate school. At Harvard, where I majored in philosophy, I studied the formal arguments that question the existence of God. Since I had no religious beliefs to counter them, the arguments made a great deal of sense at the time. Then, as the 1960s continued, a series of prominent murders shocked the world: President John F. Kennedy in November 1963; Dr. Martin Luther King Jr. in April 1968; and Robert F. Kennedy in June 1968. How could God have allowed these men to die? These assassinations convinced me, once and for all, that God did not exist . . . or if He did, as one of my philosophy professors had suggested, He had lost interest in the human race and simply walked away.

A 30-year teaching career followed: eight years at Olney High School, a Philadelphia public school, and then 22 years at my alma mater, Friends Select—the latter because I had accidentally encountered my former English teacher at a conference, and she mentioned that she was retiring. I called the headmaster, who invited me to interview; three days later, I was offered the position. In both schools, I taught high school English, motivated by my desire to help others by preparing them for whatever they wanted to do with their lives. I tried to teach my students to read critically and to write with power and precision; and when we talked about literature, I encouraged free discussion, often reminding them, "There are no right answers, only right questions."

Then, at age 51, I made a mid-life career change. It began when I happened to see a classified ad for a writer's assistant "to write lively grammar exercises for college textbook author." I was intrigued . . . an opportunity to do my own creative writing and get paid for it! Once I landed the job, I spent many weekends and summers doing exactly that. When that author started his own publishing company and invited me to join him, I waited four years to commit, during which I taught two classes a day at Friends Select and worked 20 hours a week at the new publishing company. Finally, in 1991, I resigned my teaching position to become an editor.

❖ ❖ ❖

Fast-forward to January 2021. My husband, Martin, and I were now living at The Quadrangle, a retirement community in Haverford, Pennsylvania. It was mid-pandemic, and most of the country was in lockdown, including our new home. But my work wasn't affected; I had been a telecommuter for 20 years. What *had* changed was that I was also caring for my husband, who had been diagnosed with Parkinson's.

Despite the isolation of lockdown, Marty and I made many new friends at The Quadrangle. Diana and Tom, who moved in next door in August, became like family. They loved to help us, and they did so in large and small ways: running errands, starting cars, building supports for our too-low furniture, sewing room-darkening curtains for us so that we wouldn't be awakened every morning at dawn. When I felt uncomfortable—how could I ever reciprocate?—Diana taught me a valuable lesson: "Giving is easy, but one must learn to receive." I began referring to Diana and Tom as our "guardian angels." At the time, I didn't realize just how well the description fit them.

Then, in September, with no warning, I contracted two unusual diseases, cause unknown: first, polymyalgia (its name means "pain in many places"); and then, three weeks later, giant cell arteritis, or GCA. *Arteritis* means "swelling of the arteries," and it can cause blindness, a stroke, or even death. The only known treatment for GCA is massive doses of prednisone. I had taken prednisone before, for pneumonia and for several bouts of bronchitis, but the dose was low: 10 mg/day for six days. I was on 60 mg/day *for three months*. The unfortunate side effect is that prednisone in high doses will destroy one's immune system.

So, defenseless, I caught a particularly nasty bug in February 2022: pneumocystis pneumonia, or PCP. PCP is caused by a fungus that is present in the lungs of many perfectly healthy people. It doesn't affect anyone who has a functioning immune system, but it can be deadly to the immunocompromised, as I now was.

I was falling asleep at odd hours and was also losing weight, but I had no idea I was sick. I just assumed I was exhausted from working long hours and trying to care for Marty at the same time. Still, I should have known something was *really* wrong when I lay down for a nap during halftime of the Super Bowl and slept until bedtime . . . yet despite my exhaustion, I somehow remembered to lock our apartment door.

The next day, February 14, I had scheduled an 11:30 a.m. appointment with Senior Helpers, an agency that supplies caregivers, to sign a contract for Marty's care. The caregiver supervisor, Tamara, rang the doorbell at 11:30, but no one answered. The only response was the frantic meowing of our cat, Caterina, stretching her front paws under the door as if begging for help. Troubled by Caterina's behavior, and unable to ignore her cries, Tamara called Security to unlock the door—and found both of us helpless. Marty was crumpled on the bathroom floor where he had fallen (for the 13th time since moving here). I was semiconscious on our bed, lying on my back, unable to move or speak.

Security immediately notified the clinic, one of whose nurses called 911. Separate ambulances took us both to a nearby hospital, where I was tested and diagnosed; then, ten days or so later, I was transferred to another hospital, whose infectious disease specialists would treat me for PCP.

During all this time, I spent nearly two weeks flat on my back in a hospital bed. The result: My leg muscles atrophied. I couldn't walk. I couldn't even stand up without the help of two large, muscular aides, one supporting me under each arm. I wore a diaper under my hospital gown. My only transport, other than an ambulance, was a wheelchair pushed by someone else. And to this day, I cannot remember any of the details of my hospital stays—the brain's way, I was told, of protecting me against unbearable trauma.

But finally all was well, or at least better. One month and six blood tests later, I was pronounced symptom-free and was discharged to Oak, the skilled nursing facility at The Quadrangle. I stayed for two more months in a hospital bed with on-call nursing—"If you need anything, just press the red button." Other than the occasional diaper change or medication, I didn't need anything. I was served three meals a day and was awakened throughout the day, starting at 5 a.m. for vitals checks and the first of four daily breathing treatments. I had cable TV and a magnificently inspirational book, Frank Bruni's *The Beauty of Dusk,* which my wonderful boss had sent me. It helped me put my afflictions in perspective and gave me hope that I could, somehow, overcome them.

And I had lots of time to think.

As I lay in my hospital bed, several questions occurred to me—starting with "Why me? (Why did this happen to *me?*), which soon became "Why me . . . why did *I* survive?" It couldn't have been only the medical care. This led to another question: What caused Tamara to summon Security to open our apartment door that fateful morning? Yes, I had an appointment, but that wasn't enough of a reason. She could just as easily have decided I wasn't keeping the appointment, ignored our cat, and left—and I would soon have been beyond help.

What I learned, months later, was that I had been close to death. The pneumonia had caused both my kidneys and my lungs to fail.

And there were more questions: What caused those amazing neighbors, Diana and Tom, to choose to live next door to us? And before that: How did I happen to see that ad for a writer's assistant, which led to my exciting new career? And before that: How did I happen to meet my former English teacher just when she was about to retire . . . and learn that there would be a teaching position available at Friends Select?

Maybe it wasn't a What or a How . . . but a Who.

❖ ❖ ❖

At Oak, I took the first steps (pun intended) in learning to walk again. The friendly physical and occupational therapists at Oak showed me how to get around: first with a wheelchair, which I could propel all by myself by manipulating the wheels; then with a walker. I worked through my fears of falling and eventually was able to wheel myself, or walk with the walker, 400 feet by the time I was discharged.

Also at Oak, I could have visitors: my brother- and sister-in-law, Arnie and Noemi; three of my closest friends, Lisa, Liz, and Heather; and our incredible next-door neighbors, Diana and Tom—all of whom, as I now realize, must have been sent by a Higher Power to watch over me. I thanked that Power, saying, "I am so fortunate to be alive and to have these people in my life."

I used to take my family and dear friends for granted. I know better now.

❖ ❖ ❖

Three months, three hospitals, and continued physical/occupational therapy made it possible for us to return to Independent Living in our apartment. Marty and I now have round-the-clock Senior Helpers who prepare meals, administer medication, and generally keep us safe. My prednisone dose has been reduced from 60 mg last winter to, as of this month, zero. I'm still not at full strength and won't be for another year or so. Everything takes more effort and much longer than it used to, including typing. But I've learned to dress myself, take a shower, and get around our kitchen—much more than I'd thought possible, eight months ago. I've graduated to a Rollator—a walker with a seat and four wheels—with which I can walk, now, half a mile. My physical therapists, Sara and Mike, have given me strengthening exercises and have taught me to walk with a cane. And I have faith that someday, I'll be able to drive again . . . and go wherever I need to go.

Speaking of faith: I've discovered prayer. It started in Oak when I realized just how far I'd have to go to get back to where I was before prednisone and pneumocystis pneumonia took away my legs and nearly my life. My dear friends Diana and Heather, among others, told me they were praying for me. I was grateful . . . maybe prayer really *does* work? Worth a try! So, as I was repeatedly tested—with both lab tests and physical endurance challenges—I asked the Powers, for want of a more specific designation, if They would give me the help I needed; in return, I would rededicate my life to helping others.

Several of my friends recommended the Serenity Prayer, so I started saying it every morning: "God, grant me the serenity to accept the things I cannot change, the courage to change the things I can, and the wisdom to know the difference." It didn't take much—achieving a new goal in the therapy gym, receiving a phone call from a supportive friend, reading a few pages in the Frank Bruni book—to make me feel that my prayers were being answered by Someone.

Now, one year later, I pray daily. I thank God each morning, when I awaken, for letting me live another day; and I ask for God's help in helping others. I can now focus on the good things I see around me and be cautiously optimistic about what the future might hold for my grandnephew and grandnieces. And I've returned to work, part time, doing my part to create materials that will help hundreds of thousands of students . . . my own version of giving back.

Just yesterday, I received a message from a former colleague at Friends Select. He had learned of my illness and told me, "Everyone at school is holding you in the Light"—the Quaker prayer for someone who is facing adversity. How appropriate, I thought, for someone who has finally "seen the light"—and the Light.

I am no longer alone. I feel the Inner Light within me, and I am connected to God.

Sara Walden Oremland

Sara Oremland once took an online quiz that told her she should be a teacher, a writer, or a librarian, and she has tried her hand at all three. She gratefully lives on the traditional and unceded land of the Coast Salish Nations in the Pacific Northwest, where numinosity abounds amongst the entrancing landscape of mountains, forests, and flowing waters.

Numinosity

The first time I realized that I was having a religious experience, it was both transcendent and terrifying. I was sitting on a metal folding chair in a small, drab meeting room at my university, at a student-run service for born-again Christians. The service was at its climax, and the gathered students were singing with full-hearted joy. The physical atmosphere of the room seemed to change—the air felt thicker and full of vibrations. It was something I could not see but could definitely feel. A feeling of euphoria swept over my body, and I felt tears of some unidentifiable emotion start to gather behind my eyes. I was concentrating so hard on not letting them fall that I began to get a headache at my temples. Confused, rapturous, embarrassed, and guilty, I fled the room. I was a freshman, seventeen years old. I was also an agnostic Jew who deeply distrusted religion.

I had grown up in a majority Catholic town. It was in first grade, when my classmates began to attend their First Communions, that I first found out what religion even was. My classmates asked me, "When is *your* First Communion?"

"What's that?" I asked.

"It's when you commit to loving Jesus. Do you love Jesus?"

"Who is Jesus?" I asked.

"You don't know who *Jesus* is?" they asked. "Do you even believe in God?"

"I don't think so," I said. I had never given it any thought. I didn't even really have a concept of what God was.

"What religion are you?" they asked.

"Nothing," I said. Even before they replied, I felt a stab of fear. Being *nothing* felt scary. *Nothing* means that you don't possess something you should have; *nothing* is an absence. *Nothing* is a dark and empty word. *Nothing* is a bottomless cavern that you could fall into and fall and fall forever.

"You're going to Hell!" they said matter-of-factly. They explained *Hell* to me. It sounded a lot like *nothing,* except with flames.

That day, I went home to find out if *nothing* and *Hell* were really my fate. "What religion am I?" I asked my mother. Maybe she could give me an answer to tell my classmates. Maybe I could erase *nothing* with a real answer, and then I would not have to go to Hell.

"Well," said my mother, "your father and I were both born Jewish. But neither of us liked religion, so it's more like Jewish is our culture. That's why we celebrate Hanukkah." In my family, we celebrated Halloween, Thanksgiving, Hanukkah, Christmas, Valentine's Day, New Year's Day, my March birthday, Easter, Mother's and Father's Days, and the Fourth of July. I thought of them as times for gifts and sweets; religion never entered into any of them. Suddenly, Hanukkah seemed to glow in my mind as something more important.

"So is my religion Jewish?" I asked. I was eager to have an answer to bring back to my classmates.

"Yes, but just as a culture. Not really as a religion." I didn't understand *culture*, but it didn't matter. I didn't get the answer I was looking for.

Still hopeful, I asked, "But do we have a religion? Do we believe in God?"

My mother replied, "Your father and I believe in Transcendentalism. We believe that God is inside every one of us!" Years later, I found out that my parents were great followers of Henry David Thoreau and his writings: in particular, *Walden*. They also liked Emerson and all the rest of the Massachusetts Transcendentalists. They had been married on Thoreau's birthday, on the edge of Walden Pond. "But," my mother said, "you can believe in anything you want, now or when you are older."

My mother intended to give me the freedom to choose a belief as a gift, but at that moment, all I wanted was something to define my religious identity so that I could face my classmates again. I tried to picture what it meant for God to be inside of me. I pictured a floating face in my stomach. How did God get there? It didn't really make much sense, but I was excited. At last I had an answer! I was not *nothing*! And if my parents said that God is inside of me, that must mean that I could say that I believed in God!

The next day, as soon as I could, I told my classmates, "Guess what! I found out that I do believe in God!"

"So what religion are you?" they asked.

The long, strange word my mother had said eluded me. "I can't remember! We're Jewish but we're not really—it's something else. But my mom says that I have God inside of me!"

My classmates laughed. "You are definitely going to Hell," they said. For the next few weeks, they would remind me of this every day. They would taunt me about this and other things too. I never again pictured God inside of me. Now I knew for certain that I was *nothing*.

Over the next eleven years of school, I came to feel both isolated and angry about religion and in particular, Christianity. As with any other attribute, being different as a kid is difficult. I felt isolated, and not just because I was not Christian, as it seemed all the rest of my classmates were. There were other factors that ran deeper than I even realized at the time. My classmates and their parents had deep bonds through participating in church and in church-sponsored athletic leagues, whereas my parents were odd-duck newcomers, and—even worse—non-religious loners in my small town. This was a logical reason why it was difficult for me to find a way to fit in, but at the time, I saw my classmates only as mean bullies who were demonizing me for being both Jewish and Godless.

In later grades, I learned about the Holocaust, the Crusades, and the Inquisition. In my mind, I equated Christianity with hatred. No wonder my classmates were bullies, I thought. No wonder they hated me for not believing what they believed. The more I learned about world history, the more I began to distrust religion. I was *proud* to not have one. *Nothing* was surely better than hate, lies, and delusion. During my senior year in high school. I would listen to John Lennon's song, "Imagine," on repeat, imagining a world without religion, comforted to know that others out there wanted the same thing. And yet, that feeling of being *nothing* still nagged at me. I could reject the evils of religion, but *nothing* still felt like an absence.

Even as I began to embrace having no religion, I was also continually fascinated by the subject. In middle school, I had read and re-read *Are You There God? It's Me, Margaret* for both its window into puberty ("We must, we must, we must increase our bust!") and its exploration of religions. In high school, some of my classmates were killed in a car accident, and I made up my mind to go to their funeral Mass, even though the idea of entering a church filled me with dread and fear. I stood at the very back of the crowded church, waiting for someone to point at me, the non-believer, and shame me for desecrating their beliefs. Instead, I was surprised that at the end of the service, strangers wanted to shake my hand and tell me to "Go in peace." I didn't know how to reconcile this beautiful sentiment with my other experiences with religion.

My repulsion and attraction to religion followed me to college. During my first semester as a freshman, I enrolled in a course called "Bible as Literature." The title of the class made studying the Bible feel safe. The very title seemed to treat religion as a fiction, which in my mind, it was.

The course was fun! I happily analyzed Biblical texts as I would any work of fiction. I enjoyed looking for themes and symbols and drawing my own conclusions about the stories. It felt like a game. During this time, I became friends with my classmate and dorm hall acquaintance, JD. He was a newly born-again Christian, full of zeal about casting off his sins and embracing religion. In his dorm room, he had the "Two Footprints" poster on his wall. The poster describes seeing two sets of footprints in the sand, one for yourself and one for God, and that when you see only one set of footprints, it symbolizes God carrying you through troublesome times. I found that poster to be both silly and moving: silly because God was a fiction, but moving because I yearned for someone to give me the sense of caring and support that this fictional God could give. But God *wasn't* real, and I wanted nothing to do with religion. Still, I wondered how would I ever get that feeling of loving kindness that JD said that he had from being loved by God.

However, when JD found out I was both Jewish and *nothing*, he told me, with real concern, that I would be going to Hell. Instead of feeling scared, as I did in my hometown, I felt a mixture of pity and anger. How sad it was that he was taken in by religion. How sad that religion made my friend a judgmental bigot, I thought.

But "Bible as Literature" was still fun, and JD and I were still friends, and we even co-wrote a paper for class about one of the Gospels. When he invited me to come to Bible study, I eagerly joined him. To me, talking about the Bible with him and his friends was the same as it was in class: a fun literary game. That they could believe that any of this was real made me feel sad for them.

When JD invited me to come to a Sunday service in that drab meeting room with metal folding chairs, I readily agreed. I was curious, and what harm would it be to go? I thought of myself as a kind of anthropologist. I sat at the back of the room, an observer, not a participant.

After I fled the room, euphoric and alarmed, I struggled to make sense of the experience I had had. Was it God? Every logical part of my brain said no, but how to account for what I felt? How to account for the emotion, how to account for the feeling of an invisible presence?

It was then that I remembered that I had felt this way one other time in my life. At the end of my sophomore year in high school, my mother began home hospice for her terminal cancer. I was fifteen and alone when she slipped into a coma as she lay in the recliner in our living room. I called the hospice nurse, and when she arrived, I went into the adjoining room. A few moments later, that same sense of euphoria and invisible presence washed over me. Just as I began to wonder where this feeling came from, the nurse came in the room and told me that my mother had died. What had I just felt? Could it be that I had felt my mother's soul being freed from her body? How could that be, when neither of us believed in the idea of a soul? I thought about this question on and off, including when my father and I buried my mother's ashes in the woods near Walden Pond.

Walking away from JD's Sunday service, I wondered if these two mysterious events were connected. I wondered if I had really just had a religious experience. I wondered what it would mean to embrace the feeling, to go back and see if I could get that feeling again. That feeling was the opposite of *nothing*. It was a feeling of joy, of love, of freedom. Maybe religion was the thing I'd been missing all along. Maybe my parents had it all wrong, and I had it all wrong. Billions of people believed in God—why shouldn't I?

I shoved these questions down. It wasn't difficult. Despite having many kind, generous, and gracious friends of faith, I still found that religion often could inspire hypocrisy and cruelty. I found the Bible to be full of contradictions. And I still bristled at the idea that of all of the religions in the world, only one religion could be the "correct" one and that all other beliefs were wrong. But I couldn't forget those experiences of euphoria and the questions about faith that they had raised. I still felt like I was missing something, and that choosing *nothing* was still an unsatisfying choice.

Since that day in the drab room with the folding chairs, I have been lucky enough to have experienced that feeling of a holy presence many times, and I have finally found a name for that feeling: numinosity. *Numinosity* is characterized by feeling a sense of awe, a sense of the divine, a sense of the sublime.

I have experienced numinosity in nature: in the Swiss Alps, surrounded by the grandeur of the mountains; and in Northern California, amongst the towering ancient redwoods. I have felt numinosity when I see human beings perform incredible physical feats: athletes, dancers, artists. I have felt numinosity when I am among a group of people all simultaneously experiencing intense emotions: at the ballpark, in the theater, at a funeral. I felt numinosity at my wedding, as my husband and I articulated our love for each other, surrounded by the love of our family and friends.

I may have no religion, but I no longer feel that I have *nothing* or that I am *nothing*. I don't believe in religion, and I don't believe in *nothing*. I believe in numinosity.

Neil Fagan

Neil Fagan has been a freelance journalist, songwriter, sound engineer and copywriter for over 30 years. His work has appeared in Performing Songwriter Magazine, The Leak, The Knot, The Nashville Banner, The Tennessean, *and countless dotcoms. He was the house soundman at Nashville's Bluebird Café for 15 years and co-authored* The Bluebird Café Scrapbook, *a history of the club, published by HarperCollins in 2002. When Neil isn't working, his favorite pastime is firing up his Harley and exploring the country, one backroad at a time. He currently lives outside Nashville, in Columbia, Tennessee, with three dogs and two cats.*

From Faith to Reason and the Road to Recovery

I didn't start out as a liberal, bisexual, vegetarian atheist living in the buckle of the Bible Belt, but here I am. I never thought I'd be a raging alcoholic and drug addict either, but I was.

I was the youngest boy in a family of five kids. We were a military family, so we moved around a lot. Making and losing friends became a familiar experience. My earliest memory of my father dates from sometime around 1969, when he woke me up to kiss my forehead and then headed back to Vietnam. I have no memory of him ever showing that kind of affection to me ever again.

My dad lied about his age to join the military, and he fought in Korea and Vietnam. Though I have no memory of my dad's dad at all, by all accounts he was an alcoholic and an all-around bastard. War was an acceptable substitute to an abusive father, it seemed. I would learn later that some battles stay with you all your life. Soldiers are taught to fight, so there must always be a war going on somewhere. Sometimes you're fighting ghosts, sometimes those you love. Sometimes yourself.

For as long as I can remember, I felt out of place, out of sorts, different, defective, and unworthy. I don't know if some of us are born this way or, rather, made to feel this way, and now I don't care. The hows and whys don't matter much now, but they did back then. I would do anything to fit in, to be loved, and to feel special. Long before I knew what alcoholism was, I was already practicing the "isms." Food was my first addiction. If one bowl of sugary cereal was good, then the whole box was better. And while I was never the "fat kid" in school, I also never really lost my baby fat. I had an endomorph's build: wide waist and hips with thick thighs and narrow shoulders. I hated my body. I longed to have the tapered waist and wide shoulders most of the other boys had, but I didn't. And, as a result, my self-loathing grew.

But I did have a talent. I loved words. I was a fast reader, and as early as the first grade, I was writing my own little poems. By the age of 11, I was writing my own songs. This made me feel special. The attention it brought me made me feel wonderful. But as any addict eventually comes to realize, there's just *never* enough of that good feeling.

Church was not really a part of our family life. I vaguely remember going to services on Easter as a family, and I've seen old photos to support that memory. It wasn't until my teenage years that I became immersed in the "born again" Christianity that would define my life for a very long time. My dad's youngest sister, my favorite aunt, seemed so happy and loved me so unconditionally. I loved spending time with her. I wanted what she had: that happiness and that joy. It seemed to spring from her faith, so I embraced that faith, too. Sometime during the summer before my freshman year of high school, I became a born-again Christian. Within a week, I'd written my first gospel song and played it at my little country church. I felt like I'd found my place.

Outwardly, I did my best to appear to be the happy Christian. But inside, I don't know that I ever truly felt reborn. I still struggled with my sexual identity. I begged and pleaded for God to take away what I thought were impure and sinful thoughts and longings. But the feelings never left. Sex, in general, was a twisted and tortured maze of desire, shame, impulse, and self-loathing. I didn't know it then, but that's a common response to sex for survivors of childhood sexual abuse. The few times I did have any encounters, they left me feeling dirty and despised. The shame I felt almost always made me withdraw immediately from my partner and usually ended whatever relationship we might have had. Despite the lack of real relationships, sex had become my second addiction—something I wasn't aware of at the time.

Before I finished high school, the cracks in my beliefs had begun. These cracks, usually nagging questions, were small enough at first to push to the back of my mind. However, they were never totally out of my thoughts. Why were there other religions when mine was obviously the *right* one? Why did other people believe so devoutly in the wrong religions? I met a few atheists, and they scared the hell out of me. (Eventually they would *reason* the hell out of me!) Obviously, the fear of eternal torture was not having the same effect on these non-Christians as it had on me.

During my high school years, I'd formed a trio with two friends who were fellow believers. We'd travel around southwest Missouri, singing at churches and church-related functions. My friends were a year behind me, however, so when I graduated and started college, the outings dwindled. I was a music major, but because I played piano and guitar, I had already taught myself much of what they were teaching in my theory classes, such as how to transpose difficult piano keys into easier-to-play guitar keys. On top of that, I also didn't much care for the rules of composition they were espousing. The details are fuzzy now, but at some point, I dropped out of college, moved out of my parents' house for the first time in my life, got my own apartment, and started working at the record store and the bookstore in the local mall. I met a couple who had formed a contemporary Christian band, and they took me on as their backup keyboard player, even performing one of my songs in their sets. The gig was short-lived, but it lasted long enough for me to get the impression that not everyone playing Christian music was as devout as I was *trying* to be.

Out of school, out of musical groups, and barely making ends meet, I let my father talk me into going to truck-driving school. Driving a truck had been his profession since retiring from the military in the mid-1970s. It was a job that, much like his time in the Army, kept him away from home for extended periods of time. As a child, I didn't question this, but as I got older, I began to wonder if it was by choice. My father and I were never close. Both my brothers joined the military as he had. I, on the other hand, grew my hair long and became the sensitive singer-songwriter that he couldn't figure out. Your dad is your dad—however, mine was a former drill sergeant with rage issues. Our time on the road together was short-lived and altogether miserable for me.

Just prior to leaving on my first run with my dad, I had a car accident. I was driving my first car, a 1974 Datsun B210 hatchback. A large pickup truck I had thought was parked on the shoulder of the two-lane highway was actually trying to make a U-turn. The driver made the turn while I was in his blind spot. I never took my foot off the gas, and I wasn't wearing a seatbelt. I'm pretty sure the only thing that saved my life was that I didn't have time to respond and tense up. Otherwise, I'd probably have gone right through the windshield and died on the pavement. As it was, my face smashed the glass, but my body wrapped around the steering wheel and shoved it down the column into the dashboard. My face was cut up badly, and I had a concussion and several broken ribs; but after one night in the hospital, I was home.

A few days later, I was in a truck with my father. Driving or riding in a cab-over White Freightliner, where you're sitting right on top of the front wheels and bouncing constantly, was a miserable experience with broken ribs. Fortunately, an insurance settlement came quickly, and I got off the truck in Dallas and had friends meet me there to take me back home. I couldn't wait for the trucking company to route us back home to Missouri. This infuriated my father to no end, but I didn't care. Soon I would be moving to Nashville.

Music City, USA, was just a big small town in 1987. The country music boom of the 1990s hadn't happened yet, and Nashville's status as an "it city" was still decades away. But there was still plenty of "big city" sin to be found if you wanted to find it—and I did. Dive bars, adult bookstores, and other seedy places would soon become all too familiar to me. At the same time, I'd also sought out the church that was known to be home to many of the popular Contemporary Christian artists of the time. My double life was just getting started, and it would be years before I could understand the toll it would take on me, both mentally and physically. At the time, I just thought of myself as a "bad" person with lots of things to hide.

My first job in Nashville was at a Sam Goody record store. At that time, it was the biggest record store in the city and was visited by a lot of music industry types. One day, a producer for one of the biggest names in Christian music happened to stop in, and I struck up a conversation with him. I asked him what the artist's next album was going to be like. He told me they were going for a sound similar to a Canadian pop band that had had a big hit a year or two earlier. That particular band was no longer putting out hits, and the producer's answer created another tremor in the already-shaky rock of my belief. Why would the followers of the Almighty, the greatest creative force there is, chase trends that were already outdated? Later on, I would realize that that's what they've always done. Christian music has always adopted sounds and trends from mainstream music, usually several years *after* a certain trend was hot. At the time, my own songs were becoming more critical of the church than of the world. This realization had a ripple effect throughout my personal and creative life. And it opened the door to more questions. I didn't know the phrase "cognitive dissonance" back then. But the next 25 years would be a long slow descent into my own personal hell, losing and/or letting go of virtually everything.

I bounced around several jobs before landing at the Bluebird Café, Nashville's soon-to-be-famous singer-songwriter venue. Initially, I worked in the kitchen as a prep cook, but I made sure to introduce myself to the women who ran the office: the owner and her assistant. After a year or so, the assistant announced that she was leaving, and she recommended me as her replacement. The owner agreed, and suddenly I was assisting her with the booking and promotions and writing the monthly newsletter.

All the early shows were booked by me, and I would often hang around the café to listen to the writers I'd booked. I got to know the soundmen and watched and listened to what they did. Eventually, I was able to start filling in and doing sound if they ever needed a night off.

Before long, I became the house sound engineer at the Bluebird Café. I worked that job for fifteen years, and it was an education in more ways than one. I learned how an artist can take control of a stage with just a voice and guitar, but I also learned how much of the Nashville songwriting machine was just uninspired factory work. And I learned how to drink—nightly and excessively. I honestly don't know how I drove home intoxicated for so many nights and for so many years without injuring myself or someone else. As it was, I did get two DUIs, but both times were when I was off work and had barely been drinking. Things could've been much worse.

I could fill up several books with what members of Alcoholics Anonymous call our "drunk logs." I did things I never thought I'd do to get what I thought I had to have—and even more so when I also became addicted to cocaine. I lied, cheated, and stole. I degraded myself in ways I don't talk about in polite company. I began losing things, at first by selling them for cash and then, eventually, by repossession. And as I was losing jobs, homes, cars, friends, and my sanity, I was also losing my faith. I lost faith in gods, religion, an afterlife, and the supernatural in general. Alcohol impairs your judgment; that's a fact. But in one area of my life, it was a blessing to have my inhibitions lowered. I was no longer afraid to question gods or religions or, especially, believers. I could fill up several more books with *those* questions, and several more after that with the creative ways most believers deal with the questions. I've come to call believers' ways of dancing around those questions "the old Christian two-step."

Like most believers-turned-atheists, the main impetus for the journey from faith to reason is the problem of suffering in the world, and I don't mean *my* suffering. I take full responsibility for my past. I don't blame Mama, Daddy, the world, or anything else. I'm an alcoholic and a drug addict, and I'm responsible for my recovery. It's the problem of *others'* suffering that caused the first major shift in what I believe.

I remember watching some epic sword-and-sandal movie where thousands of nameless peasant soldiers were marching into battle against another army of the same. I thought of how long this has been the history of humankind: the slaughter of young men and women whose only purpose in this life seems to be to feed the beast we call war. That didn't square too well with the cliché I'd heard for years in church: "God has a purpose for everyone!" And then came the knowledge that approximately 16,000 children die each day from starvation. Thousands more die from abuse, neglect, and disease. And all these deaths are through no fault of their own! How could this be the "plan" of some loving god?

The other reason many believers become atheists is that they read the entire Bible. Fortunately, there have been countless books written about the many errors, inconsistencies, and contradictions contained in the Bible. These books also point out just how few of the stories in the Bible are original. I'm no scholar of world religions, but I've read enough to know that many of the same central themes, stories, and characters of one religion appear in other religions. And, finally, I came to see the main character of the Bible for what he/she/it really is: a wrathful, petty, jealous, genocidal, egomaniacal dictator who must extort praise, worship, love, and loyalty under the threat of eternal torture. Nothing that *demands* worship is worthy of worship.

I renounced my faith. I freed myself of the fear of eternity, whether that eternity means heaven or hell. I realized humans were not made for eternity anyway. Most of us lose our tempers when we don't make it through the green light and must wait another two minutes. After a billion years or so of sitting around on clouds and strumming our harps for the Almighty, we're gonna go crazy. I let it all go.

But I still had a problem. I was a raging alcoholic and drug addict who'd lost everything, had to move in with his parents at the age of 40, and kept abusing substances until it became clear that the only thing left to lose was my life—something that was getting to be more of a possibility every day. My heart was telling me it couldn't take much more. One way or the other, I was going to stop.

While part of me wanted to die, another part didn't. I listened to that part. I'd been to rehab once, but I wasn't ready to get clean. I'd been to a few AA meetings, but I couldn't stand how happy most of the people were while I was so miserable. Even so, I had many friends and acquaintances who used the program to get sober, and they seemed to be living their best lives. I was finally ready to do what I had spent 25 years running from: I asked for help. I found a meeting just up the road from my parents' home, and I went. I sat with my head down and didn't say a word. I went again the next week and did the same. I was still struggling with the substances, but I went again the third week. One person said "Keep fighting it" as he passed me on his way out when the meeting was over. It takes one to know one. Eventually, I did raise my head and said, "I'm Neil. I'm an alcoholic and a drug addict."

There was no pink cloud for me. While I was going through it, I couldn't really see it; but looking back, I can see how angry I was that first year of sobriety. I ranted and raved in meetings, blamed my feelings on everyone and everything else, and said a lot of bullshit that I didn't really mean or understand—but the people told me to keep coming back. And I did. And when I wasn't ranting and raving, I tried to listen and learn. While most people think AA is built around a Judeo-Christian "god," I see a lot of Buddhist principles in the steps. I learned about acceptance and letting go. I learned about personal responsibility. I learned about love and tolerance. I'm still learning. And I'm still a militant atheist. Drugs and alcohol are not supernatural. But they were my higher power for 25 years.

My higher power today isn't supernatural, either. The G-O-D I rely on today consists of a Group Of Drunks, Good Orderly Direction, and the Great OutDoors. I have sponsees who come to me because I'm an atheist, and they, too, struggle with the belief in any sort of gods. I also have sponsees who *do* believe in an omnipotent deity. It doesn't matter to me. In recovery, we focus on the similarities. A higher power is a higher power. Outside the rooms of AA, I'll happily debate anyone about the existence of gods until I'm blue in the face, and I often do. But I'm getting better at the whole "live and let live" principle.

Today, I have more peace than I've ever known before. The world didn't change when I got sober, and yet everything is different. I still struggle with the same things: depression, horrible body image, and the desire to control. AA doesn't cure us of our alcoholism. It sure isn't going to cure me of anything else. Recovery has simply given me the tools to live with things and not be controlled by them.

And my life is good. The world, as the result of billions of years of creation, destruction, and evolution, is an amazing place. The world, as the result of some unseen, unheard sky daddy, is an abject failure. So I choose the natural world. And whether they come from a book or a bottle, life is *so* much better without spirits.

Kathy Johnsey

Kathy Johnsey is a sixth-generation Tennessean living near Nashville. Her love of words and books from an early age made her want to be a writer. She was packed off to nursing school instead. Forty years and two kids later, she has learned many valuable life lessons. When she is not writing and drinking really good sweet tea, she enjoys hiking, photography, birdwatching, and bargain hunting. Two of her goals are to write books for children and live in the Smoky Mountains. She believes that laughter is the best medicine, and the joy of the Lord is her strength. She loves the Lord and He loves her: that is the foundation of her life. Her journey of faith "ain't over yet."

My Journey of Faith "Ain't Over Yet"

I was born six weeks early. Newborn intensive care units did not exist yet. It is a miracle that I survived! I came home two weeks later, weighing about four pounds. Six decades later, I can say this with total confidence: I might have started as "the runt" (as my dad used to jokingly call me), but I was no weakling. *I am a survivor.* And God has put this character trait to the test more times than I can count.

I suppose my faith journey began as far back as 1962. That is my earliest recollection of "going to church." I was two years old, the youngest member of my staunch Southern Baptist family. I was literally raised in the church from the time I was born. When my family was not attending our regular church, we were on the road, traveling all over West Tennessee. My father was a full-time lawyer and a part-time preacher. He would "supply preach" or "hold a revival" at small-town and rural churches on a regular basis.

I grew up in the city, but sometimes my dad would take us to a state park. Going through the main gate, I would see the ranger's house. Almost every time, I would tell my dad, "When I grow up, *I'm* going to be the park ranger here and live in *that house*." He would just smile. I am pretty sure he knew that his asthmatic daughter would *not* be a forest ranger. I believe he already knew something that I would learn: God had a divine plan for my life.

I also spent many days at my grandmother's farm. For a scrawny city kid with asthma, this was a magical place where I could dream big dreams. It was here that I developed a love of nature. It was also here that I began to experience the struggles of a chronic illness: I had a major asthma attack nearly every time we went there. Looking back, I realized that having asthma laid the earliest foundations for my career as a registered nurse. I just did not know it yet.

One summer evening, when I was five years old, I was playing in the backyard with my brothers and sister. I was on the big swing set, swinging as high as I could go. The next thing I remember was my brother yelling, "She can't breathe! Go get Mom, quick!"

My dad scooped me up, and away in the car we went. I had no idea that he and my mom were taking me to a hospital. In the ER, a nurse made me take off my dress. I began to cry; I did not want to undress in front of this stranger. Next, I was on a stretcher, being rolled down the hallway. I can still see the ceiling lights whizzing by as I looked up. I was taken to another room, where there was a big black machine. My parents were not allowed to come in. I had to lie very still and hold my breath. That was hard to do when all I wanted to do was cough. Part of the big machine was pressed to my chest. I was having a chest x-ray, but I had no idea what a "chest x-ray" was.

I heard a doctor tell my parents, "She has double pneumonia." I wondered what that meant, but I did not say anything.

We went up in the elevator and into another room, where I was placed inside something called an oxygen tent. It was cold, damp, and noisy in there. I fought to breathe. My dad explained: "You've got to stay in this tent; it will help you breathe better."

The next morning, I heard the handle clacking as the door of my room opened. The foggy tent made it hard to see who was there. A nurse lifted up the tent, tucked it behind the headboard, and said, "You can come out just long enough to eat some breakfast."

Suddenly, however, she flipped me over onto my side to give me an injection. I was wiggling and squirming, trying to get free from her hands. My dad came over, took my hand, and told me that I had to take this medicine to get better. The nurse was all business and sternly said, "Be still and don't cry. Big girls don't cry!" I choked back my tears, lay as still as I could, and squeezed my dad's big, strong hand. Twice a day, during the week that I remained in the oxygen tent, I got a shot of horrible thick white penicillin goo.

I learned to hate nurses from a very early age!

But I also learned to love church from a very early age. As a child, I knew many of the songs in the Baptist Hymnal by heart, I was one of the fastest kids in "Bible Drill" competitions, and I went to Sunday school, Training Union, and Girls in Action. I heard the adult choir perform Handel's *Messiah* every December, and I knew nearly all the words to it by the time I was ten. I learned about Annie Armstrong and Lottie Moon, went to summer youth camp, and helped in the church nursery.

One Sunday afternoon, when I was eight years old, I asked my mother, "Why can't I have the grape juice and little cracker when we have the Lord's Supper ceremony at church?"

All she said was, "Because you are not saved." Then she went into the kitchen and made a phone call.

That evening, my parents sent me to speak with our elderly pastor. He drilled me up and down on God, Jesus, salvation, sin, and repentance. I could not think of any great sins that I had committed so far, but I answered his questions as best I could.

He told me about the beauty and blessings of Heaven and the fire and torment of Hell. Then he looked straight into my eyes and said, "If you die *today*, do you know where you are going?"

I didn't even know if my family was going for ice cream after the evening church service or what the sermon had been about that morning. I just knew that I wanted *out* of his office. I was pretty scared and did *not* want to talk to him. Why had my parents made me meet with him by myself?

He spoke sternly again. "Young lady, listen to me! If you die today, *where* will you spend eternity?" I sat on my hands and quietly said, "In heaven, I hope." The next thing I knew, he was telling me to repeat "The Sinner's Prayer." After I said *Amen,* he announced, "You are saved!" Then he told me to go to my Training Union class and tell my teacher why I was late.

I did not know if what I had just gone through would get me into Heaven. I didn't really feel any different. I knew the Bible story about Saul meeting God on the road to Damascus, but I did not see or hear God in the pastor's office. But who was I, an eight-year-old girl, to question the ways of the Southern Baptist Church?

The following Sunday, I was dunked in the baptismal pool in front of the whole church. I was still unsure why all of this was necessary just to get a tiny glass of grape juice and a little cracker once a month, but I decided to just go along with it anyway. The next month, and every month thereafter, at the Lord's Supper ceremony, I got my grape juice and little cracker. Mission accomplished.

Life in the Southern Baptist Church went on. The same old sermons, the same old songs, the same old rituals, the same old activities, Sunday after Sunday, year after year. I was a shy kid who never caused much trouble. I was a straight-A student and would become valedictorian of my graduating class. Yes, I was pretty much an academic nerd who believed in God and was just trying to do all the right things.

As I grew up, I started to sense that there had to be more … *but what?* I started to learn "what" very soon.

At age 14, I was molested by a family member and then by a stranger. I was too terrified to tell anyone. So I kept quiet. When I was almost 17, my brother (two years older) committed suicide. No one *ever* wanted to talk about that. So I kept quiet. I had no idea where God was during all of this or why any of it happened. These were my first encounters with "bad things happening to good people." It made no sense. I was so hurt and so overwhelmed. The only remedy I could find was to bury myself deeper in my schoolwork and my writing.

The summer I turned 17, I felt a deep hole in my life that all the sermons and church activities were not filling. I decided to do what every good, and confused, Southern Baptist does: I rededicated my life to God and was rebaptized. This time I understood how sin separates a person from God. This time the death and resurrection of Jesus, for *my* sins, was real to me. This time I *knew* that I had been born again. *Now*, the promise of going to Heaven, one day, applied to me. Surely, my newfound life in Jesus Christ would fill the emptiness that I was feeling. It did—but not for long.

What I had not realized yet was this: Satan would try to make me stumble and fall over and over again, hoping I would not get back up.

I attended private Christian school during grades 7 through 12. I had Bible class every day and went to chapel once a week. My head was stuffed full of Bible verses, doctrines, and hymns. Despite all of this, I still felt a piece was missing, but I had no idea what the piece was or where to find it.

As a teenager, I decided that I wanted to be a writer. All my schoolteachers encouraged this goal, but my parents quickly decided to discourage it. They told me that writing was not a "real job." Did they know or even understand that the world needs great writers? There was no arguing with them. I was forced to accept the fact that writing was not going to be my career. It became my hobby instead.

A few days after my 18th birthday, I was packed off to a three-year nursing school. It was not just *any* nursing school, but one of the most demanding nursing schools east of the Mississippi River. My life would never be the same again.

I survived nursing school and graduated three months before I turned 21. I was determined to be a much better nurse than the ones I had encountered as a child. For the first ten years after graduation, I devoted myself to inpatient pediatrics. Now my eyes were being opened to the hard realities of life: pain, fear, heartache, suffering, death, and many other circumstances that are out of anyone's control. Some people were praising God, and others were cursing Him. Being a part of this, day after day, made me take a hard look at my own faith. *What did I really believe?* Was I just clinging to the Southern Baptist doctrine that I had been taught my whole life?

When I was young, I used to brag and say, "*My* husband will be like Clark Gable mixed with Billy Graham. We will live in the country and have two kids and a dog." Nope, none of that happened (except the two kids and a dog). Now that I was an adult, God began revealing Himself to me, step by step, day by day, on a much deeper level. I was about to start climbing many mountains and hiking through many valleys.

I began dating a guy from church who I thought was the love of my life. We got engaged on my 22nd birthday. He decided to cheat on me before we even made it down the aisle. I gave him back the engagement ring and canceled the wedding. I was crushed. He moved to Texas; I stayed in Tennessee. Then he married someone else. Like the country music song says: *the world didn't stop for my broken heart.* I felt like I had been hit by a steamroller. All I could do was pick myself up and keep marching forward. He was one of the first people that made me ask the question: *What does it really mean to be a* genuine *Christian?*

Life was just getting starting to teach me the hard lessons. These lessons would force me to rely on God and no one else.

Soon, I was "caught on the rebound" by a charming fellow. He also went to my church and claimed to be a Christian. He was good-looking and smooth-talking. I was still pretty naive when it came to matters of the heart. We started to date. The abuse and control began almost immediately. I soon realized that there was no way out. He was pulling all the strings. I married him (out of fear and guilt) and had two children by our fifth anniversary. I hoped married life and fatherhood would change him for the better. It did not. His anger and unpredictable behavior only increased.

I was exhausted. Trying to work as a nurse, juggle two young children, keep the peace, stay on top of bills, and deal with my husband's irrational behavior was taking its toll.

Was this all that life had in store for me?

Through it all, I learned to really lean on God. He held me tight and gave me the strength and grace to make it through each day. He placed certain people in my life who became dear friends. They were shelters in the storm. Their homes became a refuge where I could hide for several hours, without my husband knowing. They never asked too many questions but always extended the love and kindness of God to my children and me. I am eternally grateful to them for listening to the Lord, obeying Him, and quietly reaching out to me. These friends helped us survive.

My husband and I separated after six painful years of marriage. When the divorce was finalized, I was given full custody of the children. Leaving the courthouse that day, I decided to focus on my children, their well-being, my nursing career, and drawing closer to God. It would become a miraculous journey.

Satan had tried to destroy me and my life. He forgot that God is a master builder and re-builder. Daily, I saw that the promises of God are true. *I was living it.* The life I have lived (so far) is *nothing* like the life I imagined as a child. The Lord has truly been my Shepherd.

Life went on, jobs came and went, and my children grew up. There were good times, hard times, happy times, and sad times. We lived in Tennessee, Oregon, Washington, Texas, and Missouri. We three had one adventure after another. Through it all, God always took care of us. As a teen, my son began his fifteen-year "atheism phase." All I could do was pray without ceasing. How would my son be able to trust God the Father when his earthly father had abandoned him?

The Lord would remind me (many times) of just how long the writer C.S. Lewis had been an atheist before He turned him around. The Lord intervened and answered my countless prayers. My son realized the lies and deception of atheism and did a complete about-face back to the Lord.

My daughter was quite rebellious during her teen years. All I could do was pray without ceasing. How would she be able to trust God the Father when her earthly father had abandoned her? The Lord is intervening and answering my countless prayers. She is still taking baby steps in her relationship with Him. I know God honors that. He never forsakes a person that is doubting, over-thinking, asking questions, and seeking. I trust that, *in His time*, He will fully open the eyes of her heart. He's a good, good Father.

Every person's spiritual journey and walk with God follows a different timeline and path. I have been through pain, heartache, doubt, fear, grief, betrayal, abuse, divorce, single motherhood, health issues, good times, bad times, hard times, and uncertain times. At times, life has shaken me to the core. Promises were broken, dreams evaporated, struggles were profound, and many questions had no answers. Fear and doubt crept into my mind and tempted me to turn my back on God and everything I believed. *I could not do this, no matter what.* In this life, my faith will be tested over and over, but it will not fail. It will only grow stronger.

I will tell anyone who will listen: *GOD has been with me every step of the way.* He always sustains me. He always provides. He helps me navigate every step that I take—even when I cannot see the path. He has never failed me and never will. God keeps His promises. Through the years, God has taught me to run the race and not give up. Whether with family, friends, strangers, or patients, my job is to exemplify Him and plant the seeds. God will provide the water and the harvest.

My mother used to say, "Life will make you bitter . . . or better." I chose early on to let life make me **better.** God is a Husband to the husbandless and a Father to the fatherless. He is the Protector and Provider. He is the source of all wisdom. No matter how busy He is running the entire universe, He *always* has time to deal with the smallest details of my life. I have prayed over kids, jobs, childcare, schools, car problems, leaky toilets, broken lawnmowers, apartments and houses, traveling safety, deciding which items to purchase, stretching my budget, and a trillion other things. I always pray for wisdom. He answers every single time.

Although God's answers may not always be what I had in mind, His answers are always the right answers. Many times, it would take a few years for me to understand why He did, or did not do, something. I have learned, time and again, that His way is the right way. His way is the *only* way.

I have spent over 40 years being a nurse: days, evenings, nights, weekends, holidays, on call—I've done it all. I've cared for tens of thousands of patients, from newborns to a 108-year-old. Each patient had a story. Each one taught me valuable life lessons. We shared countless laughs, victories, losses, and tears. I strove to bless and serve each one of them. They all blessed me.

From pediatrics to geriatrics, each person was put in my path on purpose by God, no matter where we were living. I ministered to the patients, and the patients ministered to me. God planned it all and put it into motion. My job was to go where He told me to go and work where He told me to work. My calling as a nurse was to minister to each person at their point of need.

I am living proof: *obeying God never leads a person astray. He always has a plan and a purpose.*

So what's next, now that I have joined the ranks of the retired? That is up to God. I am still following His lead. There are many more people to cross paths with, to minister to, and to share His love with.

My journey of faith "ain't over yet!"

And who knows? Maybe I will be a writer after all.

Tierra George

Tierra George is a young businesswoman, mental health advocate, songwriter, and aspiring author living in Charlotte, North Carolina. She started her first business in the network marketing and direct sales industry at 19 years old and has since expanded her skills to include financial services. As someone who has experienced and struggled with depression, anxiety, and sexual assault, she is involved in educating others on the importance of prioritizing mental and emotional health and plans to launch a new business that will provide services and support for victims of sexual abuse. When she is not working, Tierra can be found reading a romance novel, dancing, singing, or spending time with loved ones. She aspires to one day join the ranks of best-selling authors and create compelling, immersive, and captivating fictional worlds that spark the imagination of readers everywhere. Though this essay is her first published work, she sees it as the beginning of her career as a writer.

Finding My Strength

"I can do all things through Christ who strengthens me."

This was the first scripture I could recite growing up as a Christian, one of few I know by heart. Encased in a black frame with a protective glass covering, these delicate, brown cursive letters hung perfectly centered on the wall over the couch in my living room. Even if, like me, you weren't an avid reader of the Bible, you knew this scripture. But as a kid, I had no idea what these words meant. They were pretty words I saw every day, and that was all. It wasn't until I got older and discovered the meaning behind the words that they began to empower me, reminding me in tough times that I was capable of achieving anything with God on my side.

I have lived in Charlotte, North Carolina my entire life. While that never changed, my place of worship has. The first place I ever went to was called the House of Prayer, also known as the United House of Prayer for All People. It was a tall, tan-colored building that closely resembled a fairytale castle with its many towers and huge windows. There were three large crosses on the front of the building and lion statues out front, one on either side of the staircase that led up to the extensive set of doors. I thought the lions were cool. Unlike other churches, we called our leaders bishops instead of pastors. I remember having someone we referred to as Daddy Madison, and then once he retired, Sweet Daddy Bailey took his place. The House of Prayer was where you respected God by praising Him and learning more about His word.

When Sunday rolled around, I would get dolled up in a poofy dress, my hair tied back in a ponytail with a matching ribbon, and small heels on my little feet. I felt like a princess entering a castle. That and the free soul food (my favorite) they provided at the end of service were the only things I liked about going. Otherwise, I would've rather not been there. I'd sit next to strangers for hours listening to nonsense. The second we sat down, my eyes were glued to the hands of the clock, waiting for one of my parents to say it was time to leave.

On special days, the bishop would hold a baptismal service outside in the parking lot. There were fire trucks, and everyone had to wear white from head to toe. My family and I would all be squished together with what seemed like hundreds of other people, listening to the bishop make a long speech about God before we were all sprayed with water from a fire hose. Confusedly, I'd wonder, "Is this what baptism is?" If so, I didn't like it. My parents eventually taught me that baptism is about starting over; it symbolizes a clean slate in life with our Savior. Understanding its importance helped, but I still found it uncomfortable, so I tried my best to get out of attending, to no avail.

Thankfully, my mom and I eventually stopped going to this church altogether. According to the Bible, after God created the universe in six days, He rested on the seventh day, marking that day as holy. Since Sunday is the start of the week, not Monday, Saturday was the proper day of worship, not Sunday as we once had thought. When my grandpa brought this to our attention, my mom was eager to right this wrong. My dad, however, disagreed with this change, so when they got a divorce, it complicated things regarding religion. I would go to the House of Prayer on Sunday with my dad but go to another church on Saturday with my mom. The back and forth confused me, making it hard for me to learn anything concrete about Christianity until I got older.

Since I lived with my mom, attending church became my new normal. In search of our "forever church," we tried a couple of different ones, but none of them felt right. I would see people dance like they were possessed and start speaking in tongues, a language I didn't understand. My mom said they were touched by the Holy Ghost, whatever that meant. Luckily, it wasn't long till we found a church that felt like home: The Gastonia Ephesus Seventh Day Adventist Church. The "Seventh Day Adventist" part meant you were a Christian who believed Saturday, not Sunday, was the proper day of worship. That's when I learned there was more than one kind of Christian and that church could be comfortable and fun. Soon, I looked forward to it. A few of the people there eventually felt like family.

Not long after joining this church, I started attending Sabbath School after service, which served as my turning point. It was in this class that I finally learned more about God and the Bible. I assumed it would be boring, but our instructors made it fun. We'd start with a prayer, read our story of the day, talk about it, answer questions, and then discuss our answers before closing it out with another prayer. They didn't judge me for asking simple questions and always made me feel comfortable. The Bible used to look like gibberish to me, so finally understanding what I was reading excited me. I finally felt like an honest Christian.

When I was younger, being a Christian meant being held to a higher standard than others. There was no room for error. As a result, I pictured God as this all-powerful being who sat on a cloud with His arms crossed and watched and judged us constantly, which was creepy and unsettling. Attending this new church changed my perspective on Christianity for the better. I learned that perfection was not the expectation. Effort was. Rather than a mean, judgmental king, God became a loving parental figure. In this church, I worked to build a relationship with God and learned more about prayer and its importance.

The first prayer I learned as a kid was, "Now I lay me down to sleep, I pray the Lord my soul to keep; if I should die before I wake, I pray the Lord my soul to take." I didn't understand its meaning, but the rhyming made it fun and easy to memorize. I would be excited to climb into my canopy bed with my purple princess bed set and recite this prayer before nodding off to sleep.

Praying was easy for me. As long as I started with "Dear God" or "Our Heavenly Father" and ended with "Amen," I could pray about whatever I wanted. I prayed in the morning, before a meal, and at night, just like my mom.

After a while, I saw praying as more of a chore. If I forgot to pray, my mom would scold me as if I had committed a grave sin. I didn't understand why I had to pray, so unless I was around my mom or at church, I didn't. In time, I realized that praying is a unique way for us to communicate with God, like speaking through a walkie-talkie that only He has access to. Sadly, He can't talk back (something that used to frustrate me), but we can tell Him anything, and it's our secret. Praying soon became a way for me to get everything off my chest and feel better.

So, of course, my instinct was to pray when I received the worst possible news. That's when I started to hate praying, because the one time that I truly needed God to listen and fix everything, He didn't.

My mom was diagnosed with thyroid cancer.

I began to question God. If He was this all-powerful being, why hadn't He healed her? Why would He let her suffer? If this was who God was, I didn't want to believe in Him.

The longer Mom remained sick, the more my faith in Him fell apart until nothing was left. For a long time, my life was an endless cycle of overnight hospital stays, doctors' appointments, and emergency room visits. To this day, I am flooded with bad memories every time I set foot in a hospital. I'm reminded of the drab hospital gown my mom wore, the mysterious contents of an IV bag going into her arm, and the button she frequently pushed when she needed medication to numb her pain. I'm still haunted by the endless parade of nurses coming in to draw blood and check her blood pressure and the yellow eyes (side effect of liver problems) that stared back at me with sorrow as tears spilled from mine. It's all burned into my mind like a bad tattoo.

Just when I thought things couldn't get worse, the doctors informed us that the chemo wasn't working as they'd hoped, and since Mom couldn't get a transplant, there was nothing more they could do. After all the time she spent fighting, her thyroid cancer was too aggressive, and this was the end. I remember thinking of all the moments my mom wouldn't witness: my high school graduation, me moving out and going to college, planning my wedding, getting married, and having kids. Who would kiss my cheek before I went to sleep or soothe me when I had a bad dream? She gave me my first Cabbage Patch doll, my first Baby Alive, bought me my first chapter book, and listened to me repeatedly sing "The Climb" by Miley Cyrus, without complaint. As a single parent, my mom gave up everything to raise my brother and me. She may not have had superpowers, but she was my hero. I couldn't stomach the thought of losing her.

Not long after we received the news, she made the ultimate decision. Rather than stay cooped up in a hospital bed, she signed herself out of the hospital and returned home to enjoy the time she had left with her children. She even stopped taking her medication.

The days after she came home were tough. Since I knew how she was feeling, it became harder to muster a laugh or smile. We spent as much time together as we could. Life was more precious than it had ever been. It broke my heart to see her so weak. I was used to seeing a strong, independent woman who could do anything. The woman I saw before me needed help with everything, even walking. I sometimes wished I could switch places with her. But when I had finally lost all hope that her condition would improve, a miracle happened.

She didn't die.

Months passed, and while the cancer stayed, so did she. No doctor could offer up an explanation. According to them, she didn't have long to live and should have died, but I suspect God had something else in store for her all along. Eventually, she healed, and the cancer left her body.

While my mom's battle with cancer had diminished my faith, somehow it strengthened her own. Despite what she was going through, her faith was unrelenting. At first, this made me mad because I didn't understand how she could continue to believe in God when it seemed as if He had given up on her. But nothing is ever black and white. She *chose* to view whatever time she had left as a blessing rather than a curse and found comfort in His words. She stayed strong and put her faith in the one being she knew who had the power to change her circumstances: our Almighty God. I was in awe. Her strength in the face of so much hardship and her unwavering faith were inspiring. She lit a match inside me that brought my faith back to life.

Once I stopped blaming God and realized He isn't responsible for every bad thing that happens, I was able to forgive Him. I learned that life is a mixed bag. We don't get to choose what happens to us. We all get some good, and we all get some bad. God doesn't *let* horrible things happen. These experiences, positive or negative, are *meant* to occur, so we can become the person we're meant to be and live the life we're meant to live. I finally understood the meaning behind "Everything happens for a reason," which gave me a better understanding of life and permanently changed my view of religion. I embraced Christianity more than ever before, and as a result, my faith became my armor against bad times; that is, for a while.

Unfortunately, no matter how strong your armor may be, it can still crack.

It wasn't until almost four years later that I found out God was about to test my faith once more. In early April 2021, I was sitting on the couch with my boyfriend when I received a suspicious text from my best friend.

"Did you hear?"

Confused, I asked her to explain further. She then sent me a voice message explaining that our mutual friend and former classmate, Jay, had committed suicide. I could hear the tears in her eyes as she told me he was no longer here. Every thought in my head and every feeling in my body threatened to choke me to death. My throat went dry, tears welled in my eyes, and a loud sob broke free from my chest as the news began to sink in. I cried and cried, leaning into my boyfriend for support, sure the tears would never stop. After a moment of sadness that felt like forever, I pulled away from him and said, "I'm gonna take a shower and go lie down." Somehow, the stairs seemed taller and longer that day. I spent most of the time crying in the shower, covering my mouth with my hand to quiet the noise. The entire day, I felt empty. I couldn't stop repeating the same thing in my head: "I can't believe he's gone." Soon, my mind replaced that thought with a realization that shook me to my core: "My friend is going to Hell."

These were the words that changed everything.

It is common knowledge that Christians believe in an afterlife, in which you either go to Hell, a fiery place for damned souls, or Heaven, a utopia. In the Christian community, if you take your own life, you will go to Hell. It's always been that simple: no ifs, ands, or buts. From a religious perspective, deciding whether you live or die is like trying to be God, which is unacceptable. According to the Bible, my friend was going to Hell, which did not sit well with me.

Days later I decided to attend Jay's memorial, hoping it would give me closure. There weren't many people, which surprised me, but I assumed since there was such short notice, many weren't able to attend. Many of my school friends were there, as well as our former teachers. This day marked my first time attending the funeral of someone I knew personally, so it was hard. In the front of the room, the organizers had laid out many photos, awards, Boy Scout badges, and even musical instruments Jay had played. Before the service started, we were able to browse through everything. It wasn't long after the pastor began the service that I thought about leaving. Sitting there listening to everyone say,

"He's in a better place," or "May he rest in peace," was almost unbearable. If it were true that you're destined for Hell if you commit suicide, then how could I find comfort in these lies?

Most people may not have understood why Jay took his life, and while I do not know the specifics, I knew what it felt like to be depressed, which was enough. I've been suffering from depression since I was sixteen, and many times, like Jay, I've questioned my place on this Earth. Struggling to find your purpose in life is hard, but it's something else entirely when you struggle to find a reason to live. Depression can feel like you are drowning; someone or something pulls you down again whenever you try to make it to the surface. Knowing how overwhelming that feeling can be, I didn't understand why Jay deserved to go to Hell for giving in during a moment of weakness.

Month after month, my faith started to dwindle until I felt uncomfortable when someone mentioned God. Losing faith in God was something I never thought would happen. I knew my faith wouldn't be strong all the time, but I never thought it would go away. My faith was where I found comfort, so not having it scared me. Knowing that everything happens for a reason helped me accept what I couldn't change and focus on what I could. Believing God exists made me feel loved, and believing in an afterlife put me at ease because I knew that when I died, it wasn't the end. God was my compass, so when I lost faith in Him, I lost direction in life. When something terrible happened, the feeling was intensified tenfold, and when something good happened, I was on edge, waiting for something terrible to go along with it. My new financial trouble and grief affected my mental, emotional, and physical health. Feeling so disconnected from God, I knew I couldn't turn to Him for help, so I reached out to those around me for guidance.

To overcome this obstacle, I decided to talk to my boyfriend's mom. She is one of those Christians who talk about God all the time. She always has a Bible and listens to church on her phone every week. If you have a question about God, she is the person to go to, so I did. Her words helped me get through this inner war of mine. She told me, "Your life is not boiled down to a single moment." Such a simple thing to say, yet so powerful. However short, our conversation changed my perspective and reignited my faith in God, something I had been missing for months.

On this personal journey, I learned that making it into Heaven or going to Hell isn't decided by a single moment in our lives; it's about who we are inside and all the other moments. It's not about how we died but about how we lived. How we treat others, our character, our actions, and a million other things determine how we spend our afterlife. Everyone makes mistakes. The only thing we can do is learn from them and grow. God does not judge based on our failings alone, but on our victories. He is not here to decide our fate based on our worst moment; He is here to teach, empower, support, guide, forgive, and uplift. That's who He truly is.

While I believe it's never okay to take your own life, I find comfort in knowing that it doesn't guarantee a one-way ticket to Hell. Thinking my friend was in a better place allowed me to fully process his death, receive the support I needed, and heal with peace of mind. That is the gift God gave me. I will never know where Jay is, but I believe he went to Heaven because that is what he deserved: peace, harmony, joy, and freedom. While I'm sad that he couldn't find that happiness here on Earth with his friends and family, I'm glad he gets to experience it in Heaven.

Being a Christian has never been a walk in the park for me. It may feel like second nature to others, but to me, it's something I actively work to improve. I haven't read the Bible all the way through, I don't agree with everything it says, and I can't recite multiple scriptures like everyone else. Still, I'm proud to call myself a Christian, and more specifically, a Seventh Day Adventist. I may have been raised a Christian, but it wasn't until I was on my own that I fully embraced the faith as part of my identity.

Believing in and defending someone you can't see can be hard sometimes, but it's worth the trouble. I find comfort knowing that God will always love me despite my flaws, forgive me when I make a mistake, be there for me when I feel alone, offer guidance and direction when I'm lost, and bless me often with good times and memories. I believe God has a plan for each one of us, and I am genuinely excited to unravel what He has in store for me. I will thank Him in good times, and in tough times, I'll draw strength from Him to overcome adversity. After all, "I can do all things through Christ who strengthens me."

Bob Miedel

Raised on Chestnut Ridge in western Pennsylvania, Bob Miedel struggled as a student throughout his early elementary-school years, jumping right into the first grade without the advantage of kindergarten. Years later, when Bob applied to St. Vincent Prep, the headmaster told Bob's mother that Bob would probably not be able to keep up with the other freshmen. However, he ended the freshman year in the middle of his class. He then improved at St. Vincent College, ultimately graduating magna cum laude *("with great honor"). Hitting his stride, Bob was accepted at Temple University, where he earned an M.A. in English literature and an M.Ed. in Psychology of Reading. Bob was then hired at La Salle University as the director of the Academic Discovery Program, responsible for recruiting hardworking Philadelphia students who needed significant financial aid but who didn't always have the highest SAT scores. Bob and his team brought these students to campus for a summer program (with college credit) and worked with them throughout their years at La Salle. Bob finally retired after working at La Salle for 36 years.*

Opportunities to Give Back

When I first began to compose my thoughts about my experiences and how they shaped my beliefs and philosophy of life, I thought luck had a lot to do with how I developed over the years and what I came to believe and do. I was raised in a two-parent family on top of a mountain in western Pennsylvania, the sort of place where I could walk barefoot in the summer as a six-year-old, unattended, on an unpaved road to visit my grandparents and cousins; and where, during the winter months, we had plenty of hills for sledding and cross-country skiing. The top of our mountain was unusual in that it was a plateau of a square mile or so, which meant there were a few small farms. As a result, there was the farm work of mucking out cow stalls, even for pre-teens like me. While we didn't have a pony, our neighbor did, and so we spent time riding in the fields and woods. So how lucky was that? I also remember climbing a small rise above our house and admiring the vistas as fields stretched and nudged up against the forest, or climbing maple tree saplings to the upper branches and riding them back to earth when they bent.

Looking back, I was indeed very fortunate to experience such a childhood; but like most memories, the picture is incomplete. We were poor. My father worked at the base of the mountain in a "cap factory" (making blasting caps that would be used to set off dynamite), and he earned barely enough to feed and clothe my four siblings and me. My stay-at-home mom had her hands full raising us all on a small budget.

Also, life on the mountain could be dangerous. I recall the trauma of being attacked by a rooster when I was about four, funny as that now seems. Another time, I had gasoline from my neighbor's storage tank splash in my eyes when the farmer's son cranked the pump too fast and the nozzle flew out of the truck's gas tank. The farmer dragged me across his lawn and down the basement stairs to dunk my face in a washtub filled with soapy water. When I stopped crying as the stinging subsided, he asked if I was okay. When I said yes, we got back to work—no hospital visit and no lawsuit either. I don't even think I told my parents afterward, though they probably could smell the lingering odor of gasoline on my clothing.

While I loved my mountain culture, it still set me back academically. My mother tells me I didn't start talking until I was about four, and when I went to first grade at the base of the mountain (no kindergarten for me), I couldn't tie my shoes and was punished by having to take off my shoes and walk around in my stocking feet. This greatly amused my classmates. In addition, I had some sort of auditory learning disability; my hearing was good, but I could not easily sound out words or break written words into syllables. I recall crying at night because I just couldn't "hear" the syllables in words and couldn't complete the worksheets I was given for homework.

So in one sense, while I was lucky, with both good and bad luck, one can't build a philosophy of life based on luck unless, perhaps, one wants to become a professional gambler. I also realize that others don't have the good fortune of being born into an intact nuclear family, no matter how poor, and being born into a family that did not have to face crippling prejudices.

What did inspire me to act throughout my life was opportunity, not luck. Like most Americans of my generation, I've been given many opportunities through education, allowing me to go beyond the Appalachian culture and experience new cultures. I do not want to imply that I disrespect the Appalachian culture, which, like all subcultures, is unique and wonderful in its own ways and which I still treasure. For me, though, a late bloomer if there ever was one, education was the door that opened up to me a world of ideas, freedom, and change.

My philosophy of life, then, is based on the ideal of giving others the same sort of educational opportunities I have been given.

My opportunities began in elementary school, which, painful as it was at times, started me on the road to a fulfilling life. I'd like to say that I quickly caught up to the others once I started first grade, but I was just an ordinary student, struggling mightily. Still, by the time I was in sixth grade, I did not stand out as awkward, even though I was extremely shy, and I got along reasonably well with my fellow classmates. My first major opportunity occurred in eighth grade when I was invited to spend a weekend at St. Vincent Prep School, which was run by Benedictine monks and had the goal of preparing students for lives as monks and as priests. I was very religious at the time, and I came back from that weekend at St. Vincent impressed, partially because I thought I might have a vocation as a priest and, candidly, because I had a great time playing basketball and hanging out with some pretty cool high school students who lived on campus ten months a year.

When I returned to my home, my mother asked, "Would you like to go to high school there?" Although we could not afford to pay the costs of attending a private boarding school, we were offered a tremendous financial aid package. My family had to pay a dollar a day. While that seems ridiculously inexpensive today, it was actually a good amount of money for a family of seven with limited income. The financial aid wasn't given because I was smart. In fact, the headmaster told my mother when I applied that he did not think I could handle the academics.

After attending St. Vincent Prep, I went on to attend St. Vincent College as an English major with a minor in philosophy. As it turned out, in college I came to love learning, and while my first semester of college saw my lowest GPA in my college career (but still above a 3.0), by the end of college, I graduated *magna cum laude*.

Looking back, I think I was very persistent and structured, with a good understanding of when and how to study. While I had an eye for detail, I could also put those details together to understand large concepts found, for example, in the study of history and literature. I also had several years of Latin and German in high school and college, allowing me to use my knowledge of those languages' grammar to help me get a good grasp of English grammar. In addition, I was fortunate to have had some really good college professors who mentored me. One of them, for example, wrote on one of my papers, "Weak sentence—use a strong verb and the active voice." I had no idea what he was talking about, and when I asked him to explain, he directed me to Strunk and White's *Elements of Style* and to the chapters in the *Harbrace Handbook* on "Emphasis" and "Sentence Variety." His advice and my reading on the subject of style made a big difference in my ability to express myself orally and in writing.

I eventually entered the monastery as a Benedictine monk, taking simple vows after spending a year in the novitiate. I worked afternoons in an operating gristmill, but spent the mornings, after Mass, reading both religious and secular works. While I learned a considerable amount about theology, Catholic history, philosophy, and the Bible, I also learned how to live the Benedictine motto *Ora et Labora* ("Pray and Work"). Then, after having attended high school, college, and graduate school (theology) at St. Vincent for over eleven years—about half of my life at the time—I left its safe confines.

What to do? Fortunately, I had a friend living in Philadelphia who invited me to stay with him while I adjusted to secular life. I taught at a Catholic high school in Trenton for a term until the school closed, and then worked a year in a Woolworth's store in Philadelphia. I soon discovered I hated retail, and so I applied to graduate school and was accepted by Temple University, where I earned two master's degrees and finished the coursework for a PhD in English literature. At Temple, I was awarded a teaching assistantship and then a fellowship. To make enough funds to live on, I taught courses at Rutgers University (Camden campus), Manor Junior College, and La Salle University, and worked in a writing lab at Community College of Philadelphia on the weekends. I was busy and happy.

The point of all the above is that an ordinary child from a subculture of the American dominant culture, raised in a family with little money, was given several amazing opportunities to go beyond his neighborhood to experience the liberating effects of a formal education that spanned three decades.

Education changed my life in joyous ways.

In his 1962 article entitled "The Marks of an Educated Man" (today it would be titled "The Marks of an Educated Person"), Allan Simpson captured much of what I feel about the liberating effects of a solid, well-rounded education. A liberal education, he notes, is not about knowing lots of trivia, but about experiencing the freedom that comes from being able to look beyond the narrow, parochial boundaries of our own subcultures, whatever they are, and being able to consider the world from a larger perspective. Although his essay touches on several "marks" of an educated person, for me he is saying that a good liberal education frees us to think and reason so that we can make sense of the world, see its beauty, and not be bamboozled by illogic, unbridled passions, or demagoguery.

Simpson's essay stays with me even to this day. I can remember taking a class on literary criticism in my sophomore year of college. We would read a novel or short story, say Hawthorne's "Young Goodman Brown," and analyze it in the light of feminism, socialism, Jungian psychology, or some other perspective. This was a new world for me, and suddenly I felt able to rise above that narrow perspective that Alan Simpson cites. Such an education also gave me confidence to believe, for instance, that I could understand science when I took both chemistry and astronomy in college, and later, that liberation theology made sense, as did other theologies, including even the "death of God" theology that arose in the 1960s and 1970s. Education made sense of my life and the world around me. For instance, I understood some of what drove the founding fathers of the United States when they gathered in Philadelphia to write the Constitution, what caused the French Revolution, or why the presidential election of 2016 seems to be echoing the same themes that emerged in the election of 1912.

I felt empowered. With effort, I could read texts on most subjects, though admittedly the depth of my knowledge would sometimes be shallow. On the other hand, when I took astronomy in college, for instance, that shallow knowledge grew throughout my life as I read more on astronomy, keeping current on black holes, quasars, neutron stars, and the possibility of a multiverse. Even today, when I return to visit my siblings and mother in western Pennsylvania, on a cloudless night the sky is clear enough to allow me to recognize not only the constellations, but the planets and the seas of the moon.

My education also added richness to my life. When I open a door, I might think of a line from *Ars Poetica* by Archibald MacLeish: "For all the history of grief / An empty doorway and a maple leaf." Or, as I lock the doors at night and turn off the lights as I go upstairs to bed, a line from *Othello* might pop into my head: "Put out the light, and then put out the light," but I also recognize the irony in that quote since I am no Othello and my wife is no Desdemona. Or when I see a stray dog approaching, I sometimes think of Robert Francis's *The Hound:* "Life the hound / Equivocal / Comes at a bound / Either to rend me / Or to befriend me." For me, then, education enriches my life, giving me a sense of depth and dimension—and much pleasure.

Education also gave me confidence to try new things. Although I had been shy, even at the beginning of college, I learned in my sophomore year how to speak up in class and then, later, at conferences and workshops. I like to sing and can read sheet music (again from my education), so I joined a choral group. That confidence also made me believe I could attempt home projects. I needed a new backyard fence, so I built one. We needed to replace a French door, so we did it ourselves.

Perhaps one of the greatest benefits of earning a college degree is that it is a way out of poverty, and in fact most college students today probably are primarily interested in the economic benefits of earning a college degree rather than experiencing a well-rounded, freeing education. It is true that one of the results of my having earned a college degree and graduate degrees is that I eventually landed a meaningful fulltime position that allowed me to live comfortably and save money for my retirement. My wife, who was raised in a housing project in Philadelphia, also benefited economically from a college degree, allowing both of us to buy a home and raise our children in a comfortable, supportive, loving environment.

What then is my philosophy of life? Simple: Work to give others the same sort of life-changing educational opportunities that were given to me. When I was in graduate school, one internationally known professor said to me when I told him I wanted to work with at-risk students, "Oh, you wouldn't want to do that for your entire life," but that is exactly what I wanted to do—and that is what I did.

I recently retired from my position as Director of the Academic Discovery Program (ADP) at La Salle University, having worked for thirty-six years with highly motivated at-risk college students from Philadelphia, students who come from families with low incomes (200 percent or less of the federal poverty level) and who have disappointingly low SAT scores. The ADP gives these students the opportunity, along with assistance, to change their lives through education. (By the way, using these selection criteria, I myself probably would have been eligible for this program had it existed in the 1960s, assuming someone back then would have recognized my potential.) During my years at La Salle and with the ADP, I selected students by interviewing them, reviewing carefully their college essays and their recommendations, and analyzing the results of some on-campus tests, all in an attempt to admit students who had an appreciation for education and hard work.

Of course, once these students came to campus, we provided them with lots of support: a rigorous credit-bearing six-week summer program; tutoring, advising, and counseling; and an excellent financial aid package that kept them from being buried in too much debt when they graduated. Thanks to generous donors, we were also able to offer emergency funds for students in extreme need and to buy some textbooks for students who did not have funds to purchase their own, which in turn allowed us to build an impressive lending library once the texts were returned by the end of each semester. The students responded to these opportunities, and their graduation rates and GPAs helped make the program a model for other colleges. The students are mainly focused on getting their degrees so that they have improved job opportunities and the chance to work themselves out of poverty, and that is certainly an important factor; but for me the real goal of an education is to liberate oneself so that he or she can experience the wonders of the world—and the job opportunities that will follow. I believe our alumni are realizing this liberation too.

Although I do not keep in touch with all my graduates, many call, write, or visit; and, through social media, I know that others are doing well and benefiting from their life-changing education. One student and her family are missionaries in China, one is a municipal court judge, one is a lawyer, one is a nurse at John Hopkins Hospital; some are teachers, many are social workers, and others are successful accountants, business people, or computer scientists. Most are raising their children to value education, so the cycle continues.

I have been very lucky to find my mission in life and to have had a series of opportunities that helped me find that mission and to develop my philosophy of life, which is, in essence, to help others—specifically, to help others by helping them earn their college degrees. I feel fortunate to have had so many life-changing opportunities, and lucky to have been able to work with so many talented, kind, amazing, hard-working students.

Ruth Rouff

Ruth Rouff was born in Pittsburgh, Pennsylvania but spent most of her childhood in southern New Jersey. Her earliest memory of being praised for her writing came in the third grade, when her teacher, Mrs. Carlson, admired a very brief essay Ruth wrote on Abraham Lincoln. Continuing to write, Ruth received a scholarship to Vassar College, where she majored in English and minored in art history. After working as a credit and collections clerk and a retail manager, she returned to school and earned a master's degree in education at Saint Joseph's University. She spent many years teaching in Philadelphia and Camden, New Jersey schools, an experience that she believes helped her when she began to write developmental reading material for an educational publishing company. In addition to freelance educational writing, Ruth has had poetry, fiction, and nonfiction published in various literary journals. Her latest book is entitled Lone Star, *published by Bedazzled Ink. It tells the story of famed golfer and closeted bisexual, Babe Didrikson Zaharias, whom the Associated Press named the greatest woman athlete of the first half of the 20th century.*

Buddhism and Me

I wasn't born a Buddhist. Neither are most of the Buddhists I know. Most of us were born into other religions or else into nonreligious households. But somehow along the line, we converted to a Japanese form of Buddhism called *Nichiren Shoshu*, or School of Nichiren. Nichiren was a 13th century Japanese Buddhist reformer. His form of Buddhism was brought to the United States in large part by Japanese women who married American servicemen in the aftermath of World War II.

Although Japanese women, along with other Asian women, have long been stereotyped as submissive, the Japanese women who propagated their religion in the United States were apparently anything but. While adapting to American life in ways large and small, these "pioneer members," as they are called in our organization, not only continued to practice Buddhism, but also told others about it and encouraged them to practice. In this way, the religion spread by word of mouth for decades, attracting people disillusioned with the religions they were familiar with. Eventually, the mother of a college friend of mine, brought up in a Protestant denomination, learned about Buddhism and began practicing it. Then she told her daughter, Sharon, who converted to Nichiren Buddhism and later told me about the practice.

That was nearly forty years ago, and I've been a Buddhist ever since. Why was I attracted to Buddhism? I was raised a Catholic, but in a liberal, nonjudgmental household. My mother was what some might refer to as a "cafeteria Catholic"; she selected aspects of the faith she agreed with while discarding others. Although she went to church, she was more liberal than the church hierarchy in many respects. I recall her ruefully mentioning a time when her Catholic schoolteacher, a nun, whacked her with a ruler. (All her children attended public school.) Another time she spoke dismissively of celibate Catholic priests "romanticizing marriage." Contrary to Catholic teaching, she had no qualms about birth control. Besides, she had done the unthinkable (to her mother) and married my father, a Jew. It didn't matter to her that the extent of his religiosity was dropping us off at church every Sunday and then picking us up after Mass. Likewise, it was okay with him that his kids were being raised Catholic. That made the marriage tolerable to my grandmother, a staunch Catholic immigrant from Austria, who went to Mass every morning.

So, based on my parents' examples, I had a rather ambivalent attitude toward religious practice. I sat through Mass in a dress every Sunday morning because I was expected to, but I can't say that I was ever overwhelmed by religious fervor. In fact, the paintings of the Stations of the Cross that adorned the walls of our little church depressed me. Poor Jesus! All that suffering! What terrible sins had I committed (or would I commit) to warrant such a sacrifice?

Besides, my mother hadn't even arranged for me to make my first Holy Communion. On the other hand, she had arranged for my younger brother Art to make his. So just how important *was* Communion? When I later asked my mother about this, she told me that we were in the process of moving from Pittsburgh to New Jersey at the time and she had her hands full. This seemed rather a lame excuse for a committed Catholic. Not that I ever really wanted to receive communion. In hindsight, I like to think that subconsciously my mother didn't want me to fall into the clutches of Catholicism, which in her day encouraged marriage and motherhood for women at the expense of any other kind of aspiration. But that's hindsight. Maybe as the mother of seven kids, five of whom still lived at home, she *did* have her hands full. Or maybe her seeming "negligence" in my religious upbringing was a little of both.

One thing I did know was that I absolutely loathed religious hypocrisy. A case in point: When I was a child, I had a girlfriend who I used to hang out with. I'll call her Janie Mills. Janie and I played board games like *Sorry!* and *Parcheesi* and *Mouse Trap* and rode our 20" bikes together and did other fun things. One summer Janie invited me to attend Vacation Bible School at her Baptist church. Even though it was a Baptist church, my mother said it was okay for me to go, so I went. There we colored and did cut-and paste-type crafts based on Bible stories. This was all well and good as far as I was concerned. I liked doing crafts.

However, I will never forget the chill November day that President Kennedy was assassinated. The neighbors were gathered outside on our lawn that afternoon, talking over the tragic event, stricken by shock and grief, when Janie Mills trotted across the street from her house. There was no grief on her face as she blithely announced to me that her family was glad Kennedy got shot because he was a Negro lover. Only she didn't use the word *Negro.*

So much for Christian love and charity. I knew even then that all Christians weren't vicious bigots, but the hateful thing Janie said made me wary of all so-called Christians, particularly of the white evangelical kind. After that awful day, Janie and I continued to hang around together, but in the back of my mind, I was beginning to suspect that Janie and her family were, in a profound way, jerks. By the time we got to junior high school, our friendship had waned.

When I was 11 years old, my father died of a heart attack. My mother had always been depressive, but now her depression and anxiety became worse. Being a single parent and isolated out in suburbia, she felt bereft. She had never wanted to move away from her large extended family back in Pittsburgh, but my father had been transferred to the Philadelphia Naval Shipyard, where he worked as a metallurgist. So she had no choice.

Like many housewives of that era, my mother took tranquilizers, but they didn't seem to help much. She was often gloomy and short-tempered, and she suffered from insomnia. She didn't have to go back to work since my father's government job left his survivors an annuity. (She probably should have gone back to work. It might have improved her mental state.) As it was, she spent most of her time doing housework, reading, and watching soap operas on TV. She had by this time learned how to drive, and she still went to church, but she didn't seem to derive any strength from going. She no longer required Art or me to go, so we didn't. My adolescence was largely devoted to reading classic novels that I barely understood, like *Madame Bovary*, and following the Phillies.

Then when I won a scholarship to college, at a formerly all-women's school in New York State, I was surrounded by empowering women. This was the heyday of the second wave of feminism, when leaders like Betty Friedan and Gloria Steinem were challenging male-dominated views of women's proper place in the world. Certainly, there were great feminist role models at my college. Renowned anthropologist Margaret Mead spoke at convocation. One of my professors was a well-known feminist art historian who asked the question: "Why have there been no great women artists?" The answer seemed to lie in lack of opportunity rather than talent. Furthermore, women's studies had gained traction as an academic pursuit. Congresswoman Shirley Chisholm, who spoke on campus, was daring to run for president. Against the background of so much feminist ferment, I no longer felt that praying to God the Father was important.

A few years after college, I visited my friend Sharon, a former classmate now living in New York City with her husband, Ed. Sharon told me that based on her mother's experience, she had begun practicing Nichiren Buddhism and that I should give it a try, that it would improve my life. Visions of bald-headed monks in saffron robes soliciting alms danced through my head; nonetheless, I was intrigued. Eastern religions seemed to provide a serene alternative to the guilt I felt in trying to live up to Jesus, who, I had been told, was crucified for my sake. In Buddhism, I later learned, there was no guilt, only responsibility, and enlightenment was open to all. After all, weren't all the Buddhas in the Chinese restaurants smiling?

But I had several questions for Sharon. I asked her if Nichiren Buddhists believed in God. Even though I now practiced no religion, years of attending Catholic church still had a hold on me. I still had a lingering feeling of a benevolent God hanging over me, my secret friend.

She replied that Nichiren Buddhists believed in the mystic law that permeates the universe but not in an anthropomorphic deity. In other words, there was no God and certainly no God the Father. So if Nichiren Buddhists didn't worship a Western god like Michelangelo's bearded patriarch, neither did they worship the rotund Buddhas I had seen in restaurants.

Truth to tell, I was a little disappointed by this non-belief in God. But could there really be an intelligent presence sitting on a cloud in the sky? My rational mind told me, "Not really."

"What do Buddhists think of Jesus?" I asked her. She replied that he was a *bodhisattva*, a being who dedicated his life to helping others. This view was acceptable to me because, though I no longer believed in Catholic dogma, I still admired Jesus.

I also asked Sharon who Buddhists thought had created the universe. She replied that the universe has always existed in some form, and that it is continuously changing in an endless cycle of birth, death, and rebirth. There is nothing permanent except change. Since astronomers had taught us about the birth and death of stars, this view seemed reasonable to me.

But I had one more question. In World War II, Japan had been our mortal enemy. Why should I practice a Japanese religion? Wasn't it possible that these Nichiren Buddhists were former fascists?

Sharon explained to me that during World War II, Nichiren Buddhist leaders had been imprisoned for refusing to cooperate with their militaristic government. Furthermore, she said that the first president of the modern lay organization, Tsunesaburo Makiguchi, had died from ill treatment in prison.

Thus satisfied, I agreed to go with Sharon and Ed to their Buddhist community center in lower Manhattan. There I found everyday people gathered in an auditorium, vigorously chanting to a large mandala—the *Gohonzon*—at the front of the room.

Unlike the church I had gone to as a child, where people had largely sat quietly, there was a powerful energy in that room as people chanted in unison. Also, unlike the church I had attended as a child, there were Blacks and whites and Asians together. There was not a saffron robe in sight.

"We don't worship the *Gohonzon*," Sharon assured me. "We use it as a tool to tap into our Buddha nature, to attain enlightenment." Everyone is a microcosm of the universe, she further explained to me, and everyone has Buddha nature, even non-Buddhists. Sharon told me that I could chant for what I needed for my life, not as a supplicant, but by tapping into my Buddha nature and gaining the wisdom to take steps to make these changes come about. This was a new perspective for me: not people existing for a religion, but people using a religion to improve their lives and the lives of others. This is called Human Revolution. Its ultimate goal, however far off, is world peace.

Furthermore, I was told that in Buddhism, earthly desires *are* enlightenment. Rather than high-mindedly seeking to suppress your desires, you could use them as "fuel" and chant for something as mundane as a new car if that was what you needed. Gradually, as your life condition improved, you would find yourself chanting for fewer material things and more intangible ones, described in Buddhism as "treasures of the heart." One non-material goal might be to improve your relationships with others. Another might be to find the courage to succeed at a task you had hitherto been avoiding. Such chanting required the willingness to look critically at one's life and a willingness to change. I was also told that the correct practice involved chanting not only for myself but for others. Since Buddhism stresses the unity of oneself and one's environment, one can only be truly happy when others are happy as well.

When I received my own *Gohonzon* in New York City, it turned out that there were Buddhists back home in South Jersey. I just didn't know them yet. One afternoon, several of them came to my apartment and enshrined (set up) my *Gohonzon*. Since I hadn't yet obtained a *Butsudan,* the wooden box used to display the *Gohonzon,* they tacked a shirt box to my living room wall and placed the *Gohonzon* in that. There was nothing exotic about these Buddhists. One was a former musician who now ran a successful paint contracting business with his wife. Another was a registered nurse. Another was a jeweler.

Together we did *gongyo,* which involves reciting a portion of the Lotus Sutra and chanting *Nam-Myoho-Renge-Kyo,* which means "I dedicate myself to the mystic law of cause and effect through sound." They explained that whatever negative effects I was experiencing now were the results of negative causes I had made in past lifetimes. By chanting to the *Gohonzon* and studying Buddhism, I could make better causes and change my karma. As a result, I could create value in my daily life and thus help to create value in other people's lives.

What to chant for? I already had a nice enough car, but I was working at a dead-end job and feeling myself sinking into the same despair that my mother had felt. So I chanted to improve my life condition and not feel so depressed. That worked immediately. Chanting just made me feel better. It may sound corny to say this, but by chanting I felt more in tune with the rhythm of simply living and less bothered by daily frustrations. I also chanted for positive friends, which is what I promptly got. Later, when I became a teacher in the inner city, I chanted for more patience and to become a better teacher. I can state from experience that chanting for twenty minutes to half an hour every morning will make one more patient. Since I had always wanted to be a writer, I also chanted to not give up on my part-time writing career and to be successful at it. That took a long time, but with the encouragement of my fellow Buddhists, I have recently had my second book published in six years.

All this is not to say that Buddhists are immune to suffering. Far from it. Buddhism isn't magic, and it teaches that all mortals are subject to the four universal sufferings of birth, sickness, aging, and death. Instead, the practice can be described as a ship to cross the sea of suffering. Whatever one's religion, negative events will appear. The only thing people can control is their reaction to such events. Rather than succumbing to defeatism and despair, by chanting, studying Buddhist texts, and seeking the guidance of seniors in faith, Buddhists can improve their life condition and turn hardships into opportunities for growth. We call this process of facing obstacles and overcoming them "turning poison into medicine." For example, I was able to turn some of my difficult experiences into poetry and stories that others may appreciate.

I'm still learning about Buddhism. The more I learn, the more I appreciate its profundity. But the above, in a nutshell, is why I've practiced Buddhism for many years. It's a religion that strives to create value in daily life; and in my life, it has.

John Kellmayer

John Kellmayer has been thinking about death and an afterlife for a long time. Fifty years ago, when he was an English major at St. Joseph's University, he sold his first story to Fate Magazine *for fifty dollars—ironically, a story about life after death titled "My Proof of Survival." John's proof was in actuality a complete work of fiction, but he had sold his writing. John has been an educator for fifty years, has taught every level from fifth grade to doctoral students, and has served as a school principal and district superintendent. He is also the author of several books published by Amazon. In earlier years, John worked side jobs as a reporter, construction worker, and real estate sales agent. He also worked as a bouncer at a nightclub that resembled the club where Patrick Swayze worked in the 1989 movie* Roadhouse. *John is retired from K–12 education but continues to instruct doctoral students in organizational leadership. He lives in New Jersey with his wife, two large Labrador retrievers, and two cats.*

I Believe I Will See Them Again

I never thought much about death until I was 30. It was then that my eighty-year-old father died following surgery and a long stay in the hospital. Before then, my experiences with death, aside from the passing of my grandparents, whom I hardly knew, had been mostly confined to the movies and television screen. I remember that, as a little boy, I cried when I watched Davy Crockett, as played by John Wayne, die in *The Alamo.* A decade or so later, I laughed at the gallows humor of Chuckles the Clown dying on *The Mary Tyler Moore Show:* Chuckles had been dressed as a peanut and was crushed by an elephant. I felt much differently when Colonel Henry Blake died on the TV show *MASH;* the plane that was flying him home to the States was shot down over the Sea of Japan. When Radar O'Reilly walked into the busy operating room and announced the death of Colonel Blake, I felt sadness pass over me like a shadow. However, my most lasting memory of that poignant scene is not Radar O'Reilly's announcement but how the grief-filled surgeons and nurses continued to operate. Life went on.

I thought, "There is going to be a tomorrow on *MASH* without Henry Blake. And someday, there will be a tomorrow without me."

❖ ❖ ❖

My beliefs about death have been primarily shaped by my four experiences of the death of family members. And each taught me a different lesson about dying.

My father's death, the first experience, was difficult. Everyone in my family was Catholic except my father. He had been born into a Protestant family but, as far as I knew, had never practiced or expressed any religious beliefs at all. My father seemed afraid of dying. It was in his hospital room that I witnessed the only act of intimacy that I had ever seen between my parents. This occurred when my Irish Catholic mother took my father's hand to try to console him. On his deathbed, my father converted to Catholicism. I was there with my mother when the priest baptized my father and administered last rites. I wondered why he wanted to die a Catholic.

Deathbed conversions are not all that unusual in the Catholic Church. The famous playwright and notorious hedonist, Oscar Wilde, converted to Catholicism at the end of his life, as did John Wayne and Buffalo Bill Cody. And, of course, there was Saint Dismas, the Good Thief, who was crucified next to Jesus and who asked Jesus to remember him in Heaven.

Did my father find a sense of peace at the end of his life? Was he thinking about an afterlife and hoping to go to Heaven? Or did he convert to Catholicism to make the matter of funeral arrangements less difficult for my mother? I didn't have the answers to those questions—not then, and not now. Still, I believe that my father's conversion was sincere. The lesson I learned from my father's death is that it is never too late to turn to God if the effort is heartfelt and sincere.

My father's death was a very sad time for our family, but I didn't cry. Nor did my mother, at least not in front of me. My mother had grown up in abject poverty, one of ten children whose father had died in his thirties, on the brink of the Great Depression. Since childhood, my mother had learned (or had been forced to learn) to compartmentalize and anesthetize her emotions, a defense mechanism she seemed to have passed on to me. My mother appeared to accept my father's death with a certain grim stoicism. I recall that I reacted much the same way to his death. I tried to comfort and assist my mother, but my father's death seemed somehow distant and apart from me. Still, I started to think seriously about death when my father passed.

❖ ❖ ❖

My next experience with death occurred when I was 36 years old. I had been hired as the founding principal of a countywide alternative high school for chronically disruptive and disaffected students. This was a tragically damaged group of young people. For many of these kids, drugs and alcohol were like oxygen. I had never seen a group of people—young or old—in which there was so much emotional pain. Physically, they were young and strong, and they thought they were invulnerable. But they were wrong. They were as mortal as the rest of us. Someone once asked me, "What's the worst thing that happens at the alternative high school?" I thought for a few moments and then honestly replied, "Kids die."

I spent almost fourteen years as principal of the school, and every year at least a few current or former students would die from drug overdoses, suicides, car accidents, or gang shootings. At first, their deaths affected me greatly. *Death is for old people like my father,* I thought. That's natural, the conclusion of the human life cycle. But how and why can so many young and physically healthy kids die? I was never able to answer that question.

In fact, as the years passed and the death toll mounted, I became somewhat numb to the experience. The deaths of my students started to seem almost as natural to me as the sun rising in the morning and setting in the evening. The stoicism that I displayed when my father died served me well as I watched my students die. The only time I experienced a strong emotional response to the death of one of my students was if I was asked to deliver remarks at a viewing. Then my response was as much a result of anxiety over having to speak in such a difficult setting as sadness for the loss of my student's life. I imagine that the kind of numbness to death that I developed was a coping mechanism that allowed me to continue to do my job day after day, year after year. This numbness was comparable (but on a much lesser scale) to how doctors and nurses working in Covid-19 wards must steel themselves in the face of the overwhelming pain and suffering they witness.

❖ ❖ ❖

My second experience of death in the family involved my sister, who passed away in her early fifties from lung cancer. I was with my mother when the doctors told us that there was nothing that could be done and that my sister was going to die. That moment was the only time I ever saw my mother cry. I put my arm around her, trying to comfort her as best I could. Yet seeing my mother cry seemed so unnatural to me that it was almost as upsetting as the information we had just received about my sister. With my sister's death, I could feel the beginnings of the erosion of my numbness toward death, which didn't seem as far away anymore.

My sister was a strong-minded and faith-filled woman who died in hospice after her battle with cancer. But unlike my father, who seemed frightened as he approached death, my sister appeared resolved, content, and at peace. I recall that my sister once remarked that she was happy in hospice, which amazed me. I can only attribute her feelings to her great faith in God and her unwavering belief in an afterlife. The lesson I learned from my sister's death was that if your faith is great, death may still result in some sadness, but it can also be welcomed and embraced.

My mother was the next to die and was almost ninety when she passed. Since her childhood, the defining characteristic of my mother's life was her Irish Catholic faith. Her death experience was much shorter than either my father's or sister's had been. There was no long period of suffering in the hospital or stay in hospice. Having weighed less than one hundred pounds most of her life, she had very little appetite when she was dying in the hospital, which upset me. I pleaded with her to try to eat more, believing that adequate nutrition might reverse her congestive heart failure and extend her life. She would try to eat something to appease me, but I could tell that she was neither upset nor frightened. She had accepted her passing as natural and told me that she looked forward to being with God in Heaven. I cried for days when my mother died. Her death seemed different from the deaths of my father and sister. But I suppose that one's mother's death is always that way. Whatever numbness about death I may have had remaining when my mother passed was gone. The lesson I learned from my mother's passing was that at the end of a long life, death can bring peace and resolution.

My brother, ten years older than me and in his late sixties, fought his death to almost the very moment of his passing. After a courageous struggle with cancer, including surgery and chemotherapy, he seemed to be recovering. He jogged and lifted weights and used to remark that unless he "won," meaning "survived," it wasn't worth what he had experienced during treatment. But then his cancer returned. The day he died, my brother drove himself to the emergency room. I joined his wife and three children in the hospital, where we were told my brother had only a few hours left to live. A priest arrived to administer the last rites. I think my brother knew his time had come, and he said goodbye to each of us individually. Then his youngest son stood over his hospital bed and began to read verses from the Bible. I had to step out of the room as his son read because I didn't want to break down in front of everyone. The lesson I learned from my brother's death was to live life to the fullest, and when death arrives, accept it with strength and courage.

❖ ❖ ❖

As I think about dying and the four lessons I learned from the deaths of my family members, I can't help also thinking about

God. For me, death, God, and belief in an afterlife are inseparable. I believe that God has intervened directly in my life at several critical junctures. That belief leads logically to the belief in an afterlife. Should not believers look forward to death? Emily Dickinson wrote, "Death is a wild night and a new road." C.S. Lewis wrote, "If we recall that home is elsewhere and this life is a wandering to find home, why should we not look forward to the arrival?"

There are those who believe that the whole idea of God and an afterlife is nonsense. Cosmologist Stephen Hawking once remarked, "I regard the brain as a computer which will stop working when its components fail. There is no heaven or afterlife for broken-down computers; that is a fairy tale for people afraid of the dark." I imagine that Hawking would have been even more dismissive of the kind of deathbed conversion that my father made than he was of faith in a supreme being and a belief in an afterlife.

I've sometimes wondered what Hawking, whose only religion was the pursuit of science, would have thought of Pierre Teilhard de Chardin, whose work I studied in college and who has been called the Prophet of Cosmic Hope. A brilliant Jesuit priest, mystic, theologian, and scientist, Teilhard de Chardin developed a unique synthesis of science and religion, faith and reason, based on evolutionary principles. A paleontologist who in the 1920s was involved in the discovery of the fossilized bones of Peking Man in China, Teilhard de Chardin saw no conflict between the theory of evolution and a belief in the existence of God. He believed that everything that exists, from the smallest quantum neutron to human beings—living and dead—is in a continual state of evolving, moving over a period of many millions of years to what he called the Omega Point, the union of all creation in God. But Teilhard de Chardin did not envision God as an outsider, distant and remote, but rather as a supreme being who desires a personal relationship with each one of us.

Thomas Merton, the American Trappist monk who wrote the story of his personal conversion to Catholicism in the inspirational *The Seven Storey Mountain*, frequently commented on dying and death. Merton wrote, "Death is always a possibility for everyone. We live in the presence of this possibility. So I have a natural awareness that I may die and that, if that is God's will, then I am glad." Merton followed the rule of St. Benedict, who advised his followers "to keep death ever before their eyes." If we do as Emily Dickinson, C.S. Lewis, Pierre Teilhard de Chardin, and Thomas Merton suggested, then we will not fear death but use it to focus our attention on the life we live now, while at the same time anticipating our death not with fear or anxiety but with a sense of a new beginning.

What I will most miss about this life is my wife, whom I met in my fifties and who is 19 years younger. I asked my wife to share her beliefs on death and dying. She responded by describing death as a series of polarities. To her death is both an end and a beginning. It is universal but unfathomable. It is significant but trivial at the same time, as everything will end for her on this earth, but nothing will change in the world. My wife sees death as frightening but also a relief, as it will mark the end of suffering and loss. She sees death as occurring in a single moment but lasting forever.

Time is likely to pass much differently in the afterlife. What for my wife may seem many years without her husband may seem to me to pass quickly. The deaths of my father, sister, mother, and brother, and the lessons I have learned from their deaths, have affirmed my faith and belief in the afterlife. I also believe that when tomorrow comes and I am not part of it, I will see my family members again. And I believe that my wife will see me again someday.

Victoria Mikolajczyk

Victoria Mikolajczyk was born in Rochester, New York, and never strayed far from home. She wrote her first stories at age 9, under the trees beside the playground, and her love of writing has stayed with her ever since. Though her passions were in the arts, she pursued a degree in biotechnology for her first go-round in college, and she spent the next six years after graduation working in a laboratory at the University of Rochester. Even as she dove into the medical field, she never let go of her penchant for writing, and continued honing her craft in her spare time. It wasn't until early 2022 that she decided to throw caution to the winds and finally pursue an English degree with a concentration in creative writing at SUNY Brockport. With the support of her loving spouse and two cats, Victoria now studies the subject she's always yearned to study, and she finds joy in every moment of her continuing education and blossoming young life.

Love and God Rays

My relationship with God started with a funeral. It was my grandfather's, on my father's side. The funeral home was outdated at best, and the air inside was stifling. I saw extended family there that I hadn't seen in years, people who came into town from across the country. I was excited to see my cousins again, the way a child sees funerals as an overdue playdate. Then I looked at my grandfather in an open casket.

My tears spilled over before I expected them. Upon seeing his body, I was confronted with the reality of death so abruptly that I was immediately overwhelmed. My father placed a warm hand on my back, and together we kneeled to pay our respects. He prayed beside me, but I didn't know how, so I closed my eyes and pretended.

That night I listened to my family repeat the same mantras over and over again, twisting their pretty rosary beads around their fingers. I wanted pretty beads too. We all sat beside each other in a large circle, our heads bowed as my grandfather lay still, as though sleeping. The adults repeated their phrases so many times that in only one evening, I managed to memorize most of their most common utterance: "Holy Mary, Mother of God, pray for us sinners . . ."

Just before my grandfather's funeral, somebody taught me that the sunbeams that fan out from the sky were called "god rays." One day, I pointed to sunbeams ahead of our family car and said, "That's God." My mother was perplexed, having never taught me this. I had no idea what it meant, but as young children do, I happily repeated what had been told to me.

This is the part of the movie where the child begins his or her relationship with Christianity, a life-long connection deep in the heart. Life is never quite like the movies, though, and that's about as Christian as I ever got. The concept of God is hazy to me—a curtain in the wind that evades my grasp when I reach for it. Like sunbeams, it's something that I can see only from a distance.

My mother told me that when she contacted her minister to baptize me, she was refused, as she hadn't attended church with enough frequency to satisfy him. My father would tell us vague stories of his experiences growing up in the Catholic Church and insisted that he never wanted my sister and me to go through what he had. As a result of both of my parents' experiences, we never went. I was never sure how much of my father's distaste had to do with saving us from the heavy-handed discipline he went through as a child, or how much had to do with the Catholic faith itself. I recall friends, raised with that heavy hand, explaining the concepts of Hell and repentance to me and thinking, "No, thank you."

I was afraid of everything back then. At the fragile age of nine, I would lie awake at night worrying about big concepts like life's purpose and death before I truly knew what any of them meant. I feared normal things, like spiders and heights. I also feared that the atmosphere would suddenly collapse on us one day and leave us suffocating, floating away into deep space as we died. (I was a creative thinker.) I think if my parents had instilled a fear of God in me when I already held onto all that anxiety, I would have broken into a million trembling pieces.

My family still celebrated the major Christian holidays. We dressed up for Easter and Christmas, and we ate nice meals together. Extended family decorated their homes with miniature mangers and crosses. But the concept of Jesus and God never quite made sense to me. Just like at my grandfather's funeral, it was like listening to strangers speak a foreign language. I was curious about what they were saying but was forced out of the conversation by the language barrier.

I sometimes liken people's relationship with religion to their relationship with sports. I never liked sports, with one big exception—hockey. My father and stepmother would take me and my sister to the local hockey games all the time as we were growing up. We sat in the upper level and had friends in the neighboring rows that my parents would chat with each week. We booed the other team's goalie and leapt from our seats when our team scored, reaching over to high-five each other every time. Because of this, I became fond of the sport and continued to follow it as an adult.

If my parents hadn't taken me to hockey games as a child, I'm certain I would've had no connection to hockey as an adult. Similarly, I feel that because I wasn't exposed to church in my youth, I had no way of cultivating a relationship with God. I hear so many stories of people who went to church as a child and hated it, or did it only out of obligation. I wonder how many of them continued their faith in adulthood. Was it like hockey, or like my father's refusal to practice?

It was 2007 when I sat in a yellow plastic swing after middle school, twisting the chains above me in a circle while I talked with my friends about anything and everything. I stared into the dirt under my worn-out sneakers as I declared I was an atheist. I said it easily, with no shame. I had spent too many years contemplating God already. I lifted my feet from the dirt and let the swing spin me in tight circles as, with white knuckles, I held onto the chains. When the swing stopped, my world remained unchanged from how I'd left it before the words left my mouth. It was anticlimactic, but it felt right.

My sister was very mentally ill for most of my early adolescence. She was often in and out of the psychiatric hospital. It became normal for me to come along with my parents and stay late into the night in the psychiatric emergency ward, offering my perception of her current mental state. I felt less like a sister to her and more like a third parent, despite being only three years older. I have struggled as an adult to let that mindset go.

I had weekly saxophone lessons as a teenager, back when music was my greatest passion and my initial projected career path. I took pride in my performances, despite having a less than stellar school band to play in. One night after saxophone practice, I stepped into my father's car, and he immediately told me that my sister was in the hospital again. I watched the rain on the window as we drove to the hospital in complete silence. I wonder all the time what was going through my father's head that night. If he was blaming himself, if he was numb too. If he prayed.

I faced a lot of emotional neglect and inner turmoil in those times. It was hard to feel tended to and wholly loved when my parents had my sister to worry about. I didn't want to burden them, so I became the best model child I could be. I spent so much time trying to give my parents room to love my sister that I didn't accept the love I needed for myself. I know my parents loved me and cared about me while I was growing up, but in the moment, it was sometimes hard to remember.

I don't think I would have had it in me to believe in God then. After all, how could a God exist if He let this happen to me, to my sister? I was still in that swing in the playground, an atheist to my core, and even now, I don't think I've ever truly left that yellow plastic seat.

A pendulum is a crystal attached to a long chain, which when held will swing in different directions to indicate answers to the questions you ask it. Some believe it to be a window into another plane of existence, and others believe it to be a way to connect with spiritual guides and even ghosts. I think it might be a pagan or Wiccan practice, but I honestly have no idea. I've never practiced anything else.

You can ask the pendulum yes or no questions, and the way it swings is different depending on its answer. For my pendulum, a vertical swing meant yes, horizontal meant no, and a circle meant maybe/unsure.

An old friend in college introduced me to pendulums when I was 18 and at the height of my years-long mental break. I clung to the concept of an afterlife as if it was the last dregs of my sanity.

I spent hours staring at my walls, trying to find a whisper of a ghost, believing that the swirling lines that eventually crossed my vision were the outlines of the dead. I wanted so badly to believe in something, while I felt as if my life was falling apart.

It doesn't even make sense, upon reflection. How can one believe in spirits and an afterlife without also believing in God? At the time, I didn't have the desire to question my beliefs and confront the cognitive dissonance they created. The comfort of something to believe in was enough for me, and I didn't care to question the logic. At that time in my life, all I truly wanted was for something bigger than myself to shelter me.

My mother became a born-again Christian right around the time I began using my pendulum. Faith came to her in a time of great emotional pain, in which the belief in God became her lifeline, much as the pendulum was mine. She grew closer to God while she suffered. The comfort of religion comes to many in their times of need, no matter how much they attend church or pray. When life seems insurmountable and huge and terrifying, sometimes stained glass and church organs provide.

I sat on the hill by the lake where she was baptized and picked at the grass. I had a friend with me, and we chatted about all kinds of things: God. Neglect. Love. They say that God loves all his children, but I've never felt love that way. Walking into a church never felt warm and comforting the way love is supposed to. Instead, attending church threw an unsettling rock into the pit of my stomach. I felt as if I was desecrating a place considered holy with my atheism. My very existence in that space was trespassing, and no number of pretty hymns or scriptures about acceptance would change the fact that I didn't belong.

By the time I left college, I was firm in my beliefs. God could not exist as He was popularized by modern Christianity today. How could so much pain and evil exist in the world, even with someone looking down to guide us? So many have been murdered in the name of one religion over another. What God or gods would allow such a thing? Such a lack of compassion and action confused me, especially as I was someone motivated by a natural desire to comfort others, to hold them.

❖ ❖ ❖

I may not believe in God, but I believe in love. It is my driving force. I love so fiercely and so quickly it sometimes overwhelms others. I spent so long in my childhood feeling angry and scared and devoid of love that I now overcompensate. Everything I do, I do out of love. I declared it first in a social media post, of all things, and now it's the philosophy of my life. I love with all my being, pouring it out until all the glasses of my friends and family are full.

The way I love each person is different. For my partner, love means laughter. For my father, it means having dinner together every month or so. For my mother, it means late night phone calls after I finish work. For my friends, it means hours-long drives across the state just for a few hours of their time. Each expression of love is unique and beautiful, and I cherish every second of it.

One of my best friends went to Niagara Falls with me for my birthday a few years ago. When this friend suggested the trip, I sat at my kitchen table in the dark and wept. For so long I had poured love into the cups of people that failed to refill my own. My parents had to take care of my sister first, and I hadn't had a close friend in years that loved me enough to reciprocate. Here was someone who loved me, who wanted to show me that love, and who was willing to put the effort in. The memories aren't as sharp as they once were, but I remember snapshots: the Falls, a creek, a kitschy restaurant keepsake, and a lot of "thank-you's." I said "thank you" over and over again. "I love you" was the unspoken meaning behind each one. I think my friend understood what I meant.

I was on my way to the hair salon one evening when I noticed a huge, beautiful rainbow stretching across a golden sky. I stopped in my tracks and reached for my cell phone, eager to take a picture that would pale in comparison to the real thing. I stared up into that rainbow for so long that I felt dizzy when I looked back down. When my vision leveled out, I caught the eyes of a stranger: a woman who smiled at me because she understood that we had just shared a moment without even realizing it. I smiled back, and my eyes swept the parking lot to find half a dozen other strangers, all staring at the same rainbow. Pink and orange melted together between the clouds, painted in sweeping strokes by the ocher brush of Autumn. It was one of the most beautiful rainbows I've ever seen.

There was peace there, a belonging that felt comforting and warm. I wonder sometimes if that is the feeling people get when they go to church—the feeling that we are in this together, experiencing life as a united front of scared little kids looking for meaning on their bedroom ceilings. When I walk into a church now, I feel only uneasy. Maybe that will change one day, the way it changed for my mother. Maybe it won't. I think I'm okay, either way.

I checked my cell phone while I was writing this and realized that there are "god rays" on my background photo. It's a picture of me and my partner on our wedding day, with the sunset bursting from behind our darkened figures as we lean in for a kiss. Out of all the beautiful wedding photos taken that day by a professional photographer, it was this picture, taken on a low-end cell phone camera, that won out. I believe it encapsulates everything I want to say about my faith—that love, ultimately, matters so much more to me than what gods are in the sky.

That moment was as close to heaven as I may ever get, and I treasure that tranquility like I treasure a good bite of chocolate or a trill from my talkative cat. My life is rich without riches, and it is heavenly without heaven. There is divinity in our collective breaths, and that's all the meaning little twelve-year-old me on the playground needed to feel at peace with our chaotic, terrifying, tremendous planet.

I hope you see a sunbeam sometime soon and instead of God, you think, "Wow, life is beautiful." I hope you think of the people you love and why.

Deborah Grandinetti

A native New Yorker raised in suburban New Jersey, Deborah Grandinetti soon revealed a fascination with spirituality; in the early primary grades, she eagerly read children's biographies of the Catholic saints. She graduated from Boston University with a degree in journalism and spent the first two decades of her career working as a writer/editor for newspapers, magazines, and books. After helping Rodale Press develop a best-selling book on mind/body healing, Deborah became interested in youth development. She taught meditation and ethics to children and teens; completed graduate courses in contemplative education; and, in time, found a position that enabled her to mentor gifted college-bound urban youth. Deborah has continued as a youth mentor since 2008. Her passion is helping young people discover their gifts, talents, and most promising career path.

Purpose, Passion . . . and Patience

"For I know the plans I have for you," declares the Lord, "plans to prosper you and not harm you, plans to give you hope and a future." *(Jeremiah 29:11)*

I need to tell you two things first, or else the rest of this won't make sense.

Let's start with my parents. If you step into their immaculate, three-bedroom condo in a retirement village bordering a golf course, you'll notice one thing immediately: my mom's decorating style. I call it . . . Early American convent. Yup, crucifixes, religious tapestries, and angel figurines *everywhere.* During the Christmas season, even the top of the toilet tank in an upstairs bathroom is adorned with a small crèche.

Second, I'm a closet mystic. Not the full-blown variety that can prophesize or part the waters or anything like that, but one who—even with all my faults and intractable bad habits—does fit the first definition you'll see pop up on Google, when you enter the search terms **mystic—definition**:

> "*A person who seeks by contemplation and self-surrender to obtain unity with or absorption into the Deity or the absolute, or who believes in the spiritual apprehension of truths that are beyond the intellect.*"

But I'm not the old-fashioned kind. Rather, I am one of a new breed of mystics: those who seek to be effective *in* the world—not only to help alleviate suffering, something mystics have always done; and not only to serve the Divine Beloved in all (a purpose the late Mother Theresa embodied with all of her being); but also to cooperate more deeply with Life, in its relentless drive to unfold more complex, higher and fuller expressions of Life. Modern science tells us that this evolution has been ongoing for nearly 14 billion years. My own understanding of what happened just prior to the Big Bang is that God apparently thought it would be nice to have company. And so, with great force of will and infinite intelligence, He set into motion a plan for a continuously unfolding Creation.

When I see the giftedness of many youth today and when I hear biotech experts like Juan Enriquez ask, in his talk for T.E.D., "Will Our Kids Be a Different Species?" I see Life continuing its evolutionary march forward well past my own expiration date. And I feel strongly my own desire to help these teens and young adults develop the best that's inside them, so they, too, can contribute to a better world.

How did I come to this view? Well, that's a *story.* The truth is that my worldview has unfolded over a number of distinct stages.

The foundations were set down early, probably before I reached the age of eight. I was influenced as much by what I read, and what the stories evoked in me, as by the typical familial and cultural influences. But let's start with the latter.

My grandfathers and maternal grandmother were Italian immigrants who were raised Catholic in the traditional Italian, old-school way. Each came in into the country through Ellis Island. (My paternal grandmother was born in America; she was the daughter of Italian immigrants.)

My maternal grandfather, Andrew, headed north to Pittsfield, Massachusetts. He served in World War I, guarding the gold at Fort Knox, then worked as a cook and then a factory foreman until an accident made it impossible for him to work any more. By that point, he and his wife, Jenny, had twelve children. My mother was the seventh. They were a deeply devout family, and on occasion, a parish priest or one of the nuns could be seen at the family table, sharing the Sunday meal of spaghetti, meatballs, and bread.

My paternal grandfather, Benito, headed to Sheepshead Bay, Brooklyn, and eventually opened a beauty salon on Avenue U. He and his wife, Marie, had one child. They had their struggles with money, too. Despite that, my father was able to go to Brooklyn Polytechnic Institute, where he graduated with a degree in civil engineering. Factory Mutual hired him straight out of college and sent him to its Massachusetts office for training. It was there he met my mother, who was working as a secretary for Factory Mutual. After a period of courtship, they married and moved into a small apartment in Brooklyn in the same building where my paternal grandparents lived.

And it was there that my twin brother, Michael, and I grew from infancy to toddlerhood, not only under the watchful eye of my parents and grandparents, but also under the gaze of the Christ figure that looked out at us from the big crucifix on the wall, and of the Blessed Mother, in the form of an exquisite porcelain white Hummel figurine that sat on top of my parent's dresser. In that figurine, Mary looks down lovingly upon the haloed infant on her lap. When I was old enough to raise my head and crawl on the floor, I could look up at her beautiful face and see her smiling down upon Baby Jesus and me.

To me, she was more than a statue. And Jesus was more than a plastic figurine on a slab of wood. Rather, he was the Friend who watched me in my crib and soothed me when the adults got too loud or the tension in the small apartment got intense. My grandmother, Marie, a physically big and domineering woman, was not kind to my mother. She considered her a hick from the sticks who was "not good enough" for her only son. She often criticized my mother's "backward" ways. Even as a young child, I could feel my mother's hurt and frustration. And I could feel some tension between my parents, too. My mother mostly held her tongue, but inside, she was seething.

When I was three, my mother became pregnant again, this time with my brother, Stephen. Soon after, my parents found a house for us in Staten Island. Once we settled into the new neighborhood, my father became a trustee of Holy Child, a new parish that was being formed because the Catholic community in the area had grown to the point where that was needed. He helped to raise money for the church that would be built—and in the meantime, we attended Mass in a movie theatre that Holy Name rented out on Sunday mornings. When my brother and I came of age, we started school at Our Lady Star of the Sea.

When I was in first grade, Sister Benjamin taught me to read. And that opened up the world to me.

Reading came naturally. By the end of first grade, I was reading at a third-grade level. My teachers put me into an advanced reading program. And they encouraged me to read *a lot* at home. As a new reader, I developed a strong interest in children's biographies of the Catholic saints. Once I got started, I simply *inhaled* them. I sped through the collection in the school library, and then my mother brought me to the public library to find more. It wasn't long before I finished those, too. And then, when there were no more to be found, I became just as obsessed with reading folktales and myths from around the world.

The saints—Francis, Clare, Thérèse of Lisieux, Anthony of Padua, John of the Cross, Catherine of Sienna, Catherine of Genoa, Teresa of Avila—taught me what it was to live with passionate intensity and purpose. Their love for God was so *primary.* The folk tales introduced me to the collective wisdom and moral leanings of cultures around the world. Over time, through my reading, I came to see that there was a way of being in the world that fit who I was inside, even if it didn't conform to what I saw in the "real world" where most people I knew were intent on getting ahead. For them, God fit neatly into a box called "Sundays."

❖ ❖ ❖

It was in high school and college that I began to connect with people who looked to make a difference beyond the small circle of home, family, job. By that time, my family had moved even further west to Sayreville, New Jersey, a mostly working-class town that had grown up around the Sayre Brick Company. Our new home parish was Our Lady of Victories.

Through the CYO (Christian Youth Organization) of Our Lady of Victories, I came to meet Deacon Greg, who was on his way to becoming a Catholic priest. He was young and fun. He resembled John Denver, and he played the guitar, too, as I did during that time.

It was the mid-1970s, and abortion was a big issue for Catholics. Deacon Greg thought it would be a good idea to put together a teen speakers' group, so that teens from our parish could educate teens from other parishes, particularly in poorer neighborhoods, about how sex leads to pregnancy and about the need to be careful and prevent unplanned pregnancies. The point was to prevent abortions, rather than protest at clinics and harass women who sought services from them.

It sounded good to me, so I signed on for the training. Several others from my CYO did as well. We wrote our own talks, rehearsed, got feedback, and refined them. When we were polished enough, Deacon Greg set up speaking dates for us at parishes throughout the state of New Jersey and drove us to our speaking engagements.

I still remember spending the evening of my sixteenth birthday in a bad neighborhood in Trenton, talking to mostly Hispanic teens in a church hall. Afterward, we sat down to a dinner of rice and beans—and my first tongue-burning hot pepper—prepared by the kind ladies of the parish.

❖ ❖ ❖

By training us as speakers and finding venues for us to speak, Deacon Greg had given each of us a sense of "agency" in the world. He showed us that we could take a well-conceived idea into the community and contribute to the welfare of others. The speaking engagements built my confidence. I soon learned to sense when the teens in the audience were listening, and also when I had "lost them," a signal that it was time to either stop talking or take the talk in another direction.

The project also opened my eyes to the fact that not all young people had grown up with the same advantages I had: a caring, intact family with a good income; a nice home in a safe neighborhood; good local schools in attractive, well-maintained buildings.

Being part of the parish helped expand my world in another way. During the tail end of the Vietnam War, our parish decided to adopt a Vietnamese family (actually an extended family group with grandparents and aunts and uncles) who had fled the country. At the time, I was part of a group of teen girls who stayed after the last Mass had ended and helped count the collection and get it ready for the bank. One Sunday in October, we got to talking about the family and about how nice it would be to bring a freshly cut Christmas tree to them and decorate it with them.

Pastor Dalton liked the idea, so he ran it by the family, and they said okay. Shortly, afterward, something tragic happened. The youngest child, a boy named Ming, was playing outside the apartment complex when a car struck him. He died that same day.

When we heard that, it made us so sad. We realized how crushing a loss that must have been, especially after all the family had gone through. These were educated people, pharmacists in Vietnam, who now had to start back at the bottom again.

I was sure the family would cancel on us—but no. We were told that they still wanted to go ahead in Ming's honor. They were Buddhist, and they believed that Ming would be able to see the tree from where he was, in the Spirit world. When we arrived, they showed us a photo of Ming, a darling young boy with dark hair and bright eyes, and they set it down on a shelf so it faced the Christmas tree. We tried our best to keep a conversation going as we decorated the tree, but most of the family members spoke English only haltingly.

Fortunately, a few of us had brought our guitars. (Several of us played in the church folk group; I was studying classical guitar as well.) One of the older boys in the Vietnamese family then brought out his guitar. He had learned to play it when he was staying in the refugee camp. In fact, he had listened to the radio so often he could play by heart a lot of the American songs then popular with youth.

When we started making music together, the mood changed completely. It was one of joy and connection. It didn't matter that the "other" had come from a different country, practiced a different religion, or spoke a different language. There was still a common chord.

During my summers home from college, I volunteered for a nonprofit called Hand-in-Hand. Its purpose was to increase acceptance of the mentally handicapped in the wake of legislation mandating de-institutionalization. Hand-in-Hand was started by two family men, Dave and Rich. Hand-in-Hand put on an annual festival on the grounds of Middlesex Community College. Essentially, they'd bring mentally handicapped children and young adults to the grounds on Festival Day, pair each of them with a waiting volunteer, and send them off to have fun together. On that day, the grounds were packed with colorful food stands and activity booths. If you were a volunteer, you and your "guest" could make balloon animals, get your faces painted, do a bean bag toss for prizes, and get your fill of great summer cookout-style food. It was terrific fun and a creative way to boost community awareness and foster acceptance.

During my sophomore year, I was fortunate enough to get a work-study grant for the summer. The folks who ran the program at Boston University told me I could bring it to the nonprofit of my choice. So I chose Hand-in-Hand, and that summer, I worked as its only paid member. I learned a lot from Dave and Rich. They showed me what was possible when two individuals, each with full-time jobs, decide to make focused use of their leisure hours in a way that brought the community together to address an important social issue.

And in college, I was one of the beneficiaries of a Washington, D.C., Congressional internship program started by a philanthropic couple who wanted to make college students more sympathetic to the plight of African Americans in the United States. The program placed one student each in the office of a member of the Black Congressional Caucus. I was placed with John Conyers, a Democrat from Michigan. (Rosa Parks worked in his Detroit office before she died.)

The last semester of my senior year, I moved from Boston into program housing on Capitol Hill. My roommate, Debra Viadero, was also a journalism major. We were excited about the internship because we knew it would help us get a deeper understanding of how government really works. But it did more than that. It also gave us an up-close look at Black culture. (The Washington, D.C. offices of members of the Black Congressional Caucus were staffed with mostly African Americans, as mine was. John Conyers, in particular, received in-office visits from Dizzy Gillespie, Bill Cosby, and Eartha Kitt when I worked there.) It also gave us a deeper understanding of how the issue of race played out in the United States. In that way, the program accomplished what its sponsors intended.

❖ ❖ ❖

All of these opportunities—the Right-to-Life speaker program, the memorable evening with the Vietnamese refugee family, the work with Hand-in-Hand, the internship in Washington, D.C.— helped me develop empathy for individuals beyond my immediate familial and social circle. They also taught me that it's possible to go beyond that moment of empathy and do something meaningful, however small, to contribute toward the welfare of others.

❖ ❖ ❖

With the "social reformer" aspect of me now a bit more awake, Life began to unfold a new aspect, one much more internal. That phase started around the time I was finishing college. By that time, my mom had come to know very well an unusual woman in our town. Her name was Nancy Gallo, a chain-smoking, self-identified religious mystic, and she gave psychic readings. In one of those readings, she told my mom that my brothers (there were now three) would all be successful in business, but that I was on a different path, one "chosen by God." And then she added something curious that has since proven true: "Mary Ann," she said, addressing my mother. "There ain't no way I'm going to lie to her. It will *not* be easy."

I didn't appreciate it when Nancy told my mother to dissuade me from going into the Peace Corps, something I was exploring. "Your daughter's too sensitive," Nancy said. "She takes things too much to heart. She'll see all the suffering, and it will literally make her sick."

But then she opened another door. In 1983, she organized a religious tour of Marian shrines in Italy. My father had little interest in going, so he sent me to accompany my mother. And it was there, on the soil of my ancestors, in the country that had given rise to so many of the Catholic saints I had read about as a child, that something deeper in me stirred.

That first night in Milan, I had a dream that gave me a broad sense that my deeper purpose was to help bring the "spiritual" into the material plane. How, I did not know. In Assisi, I had a vision in which the cathedral I was in dissolved into nothingness before my eyes, and what came into view in its place was a scene in which Franciscan monks were gathered in an open-air marketplace. I suddenly felt drawn into their midst. I could hear them talking, and I could smell the odors of the goods in the market. It lasted but a few moments, and then the interior of the cathedral came back into view, just as the tour guide was pointing out where in the cathedral space St. Francis had built his initial chapel, with his own hands. In Loretto, I had another vision, this time of Jesus and his mother, Mary, ascending a staircase. One of them—and I can't remember which—looked over their shoulder at me and beckoned me to follow. And in Rome, standing in front of the Basilica and hearing the bells ring out, I had a strong inner sense that the Blessed Mother was calling me to do some work on her behalf. What it was, I did not know.

It would take the next three decades to gain clarity. During those years, I worked in newspaper and magazine journalism and then book publishing. My work took me from the Lehigh Valley in Pennsylvania, to Los Angeles, then up north to Sonoma, then back again to the East Coast. On my own time, I explored the philosophies and practices of several of the world's mystical traditions: Buddhism, Sufism, Native American spirituality, Vedic/Hindu spirituality, and later, the Kabbalistic teachings. I also read biographies and autobiographies of Catholic saints, such as Thérèse of Lisieux's *Story of a Soul.* And, just as I had felt compelled, as a child, to read as much as I could about the Catholic saints, I now felt pulled to understand the tenets all true religions have in common. During this period, I meditated just about every day, often morning and evening. I found myself praying to become a clear vessel, another channel through which God's love might touch the world. Emotionally, I went through a kind of purging and purification. And then, around 1996 or 1997, I was at the New York yoga center I attended regularly and heard an announcement that they were looking for volunteers to teach the children's meditation program. I was immediately attracted. I had already sensed, in the aftermath of certain of my deeper meditations, that I would someday work with children. And that one day, my work might extend to children around the world.

I signed up, got trained, and got to it. It didn't take long before I knew that this was what I was meant to do: support children and teens in bringing the highest and best in themselves into being. Doing that as a volunteer was satisfying for a while. And then I started to feel that I wanted to do this as my regular work. I didn't know what that would look like, however. I considered going to graduate school to become a high school teacher, but that didn't feel right. I was a writer, and I could have gotten my master's degree and taught high school English. But that's not what I was after.

For much of the next decade, I tried to figure it out. I looked for opportunities in the newspaper and online. I wrote a proposal to the John Templeton Foundation, which got me an invitation to do a single project, a review of an initiative they had underway on creating an academic course of study on spiritual formation in children. But that's as far as I went. I continued to visualize what I wanted and to talk to God. Boy, did I talk to God about what I wanted. All the while, I continued as a volunteer meditation teacher. When my work took me to Running Press Book Publishers in Philadelphia, I started a children's meditation program in the affiliate yoga center there.

Eventually, I got a one-year contract job as the publications coordinator for the Center for Afterschool Education at Foundations in Moorestown, New Jersey. I hadn't realized that there was this whole other sphere in education that could address the nonacademic aspects of children's development that were not adequately met in school. Now I was getting somewhere. The folks there, the best in the field at the time, trained teachers and promoted best practices in out-of-school-time learning, especially for English language learners.

When that job ended, the first decent job I could find was another publishing job with a company that produced educational books for nurses. I was bored out of my mind and knew I had to do something different, so I applied to a graduate program in Contemplative Education at Naropa University. Part of it was taught online; the other part required on-campus attendance at a summer seminar. It was designed for teachers who had the summer off. I begged my boss to let me take an extended (unpaid) summer vacation the first year and completed one year of the program. But layoffs at the company severely reduced the workforce after that, so there was no way I could go back the following summer. The program simply wasn't a good fit for someone who worked year-round in publishing.

Meanwhile, I persisted in looking for work that would give me the opportunity to use the skill set and understanding I was building regarding youth development. And then, one day, I saw a small ad on Craigslist. An educational publisher was looking for a mentor for Camden youth. I poured my heart into my letter of introduction. Soon afterward, I found myself sitting down to dinner with that publisher, who told me that he and his wife had a strong desire to become very good neighbors to the children of Camden. They had created, with profits from their business, their own foundation to fund their initiatives. My skill set seemed to be a good match for some of the projects they had underway.

The dinner, by the way, was in an *Italian* restaurant.

I should have known that was a clue that my prayers were about to be answered.

❖ ❖ ❖

In late 2007, I strongly felt the call of the children in Camden. I resigned my editing job, even though I didn't have much in the way of savings or even a solid plan about how to support myself without a fulltime job. Financially, I put myself in a *scary* position. (In fact, I never told my parents that I had resigned, because they would have said I was being extremely irresponsible and reminded me that God *wouldn't* pay my rent.) This was a time of learning to trust God and not second-guess myself. It was also a time for learning that God, rather than any job, was the source of good (and income) in my life. Slowly, the work did come in—some freelance book editing and a very welcome opportunity from the foundation to teach, on a part-time basis, GED-style material in a community learning center in Camden. Financially things were tight, but even when I broke my wrist and had to put aside my writing work for a little while, I never went without food. God *always* came through. And while my parents weren't happy that I was now free-lancing, they generously offered to help with the larger, one-time expenses, like dental surgery.

Eventually, the couple who started the foundation asked me to mentor a group of gifted students from Camden who were attending Camden Catholic High School on partial scholarships the foundation had provided. This was the opening I had prayed for over the years, not with a specific prayer, but with one that in which I asked God to "create for me now paying work that will not only serve the community in the way it most needs to be served, but also help my soul to grow in the way it most needs to grow. May the work bring me joy and more than enough income to meet my needs."

These teens, who had endured so much hardship, inspired me. They were irrepressible. They had such a thirst for new experiences. They easily drew forth my best. When I spent time with them, I felt the outflowing of a love that was pure, that had no agenda beyond wanting the best for them. That was the kind of love I felt flow into me in deeper states of meditation, and now, with these teens, it had found an outlet beyond me. In that connection, I felt a sense of completion.

Whether we are aware of it or not, Life is always calling us to take the next step, to become more of who we were created to be. I've come to see that people are like diamonds with many facets, each being revealed and polished in turn. So few see themselves for the gems that they are, or even fully understand the way in which the forces in their lives are converging to shape them into something even more beautiful.

What five decades of living has taught me is that God does have a plan for our lives. And it is a *very good* one.

Harry Taylor

Harry Taylor was born and raised in northern New Jersey, earned a BA from Colgate University, and served in the U.S. Air Force. He spent 20 years in Colorado—mostly in the mountains—where he began a long career in commercial real estate and development. He relocated to Charlotte, North Carolina in 1987. In addition to devoting time and energy to such youth programs as Big Brothers, Habitat for Humanity, Communities in Schools, and Outward Bound, Harry has been an environmental and community activist. In 2008, Harry ran for the U.S. House of Representatives. Frustrated with elections tainted by gerrymandered districts, he began speaking publicly about redistricting reform in early 2009 and went on to write a book, You Can't Get There from Here, *that describes the challenge of running for public office when election outcomes are pre-rigged by political parties. He is an active volunteer with Common Cause, Democracy North Carolina, and the League of Women Voters. For relaxation, Harry plays banjo, fiddle, and mandolin. An avid fisherman since the age of 8, he is also a skilled skier, rock-climber, and whitewater kayaker; and he continues to play tennis and ride copious miles on his bike. He hasn't owned a TV for decades; instead, he reads extensively.*

Bridge Building

A boy of perhaps five or six years lies propped on his elbows on the carpeted floor of his grandmother's small sunroom. There are windows on three walls; on the fourth, a door to the living room. Bookshelves straddling the door—two tiers high—are packed tight with decades of *National Geographic* magazines.

An issue is open before him, and though he's not yet a reader, the photos and maps fascinate him. Two adult uncles still "live at home" and sit nearby. Safely back from World War II stints in the Army Air Corps and Navy, they are the ones who read *National Geographic* cover to cover each month. Their bottomless knowledge, much of it gleaned from that publication, always fascinates the kid. With an uncommon curiosity, he too would become a lifelong reader, experiencing different people, places, dialects; mountains, oceans, rivers, buildings; fish and polar bears; space flights, wars, disease, county fairs and banjo players; even cutaway diagrams of King Tut's sarcophagus and sunken ships.

I am that boy—the first of four; numbers two and three followed a few years apart. Shortly after my fifth birthday, we lost our mother to breast cancer. Within a year, our father would remarry, and brother number four made his entry. We acquired a new mom, a third set of grandparents, a new cast of aunts, uncles, and cousins. Lots of competition for attention ensued, with the oldest—that's me—often left to wander, explore, and figure things out by my own wits. There's little surprise that I'm something of a loner, and with an independent streak right out of the box.

My dad's parents were able to afford domestic help—cook, maid, chauffeur, gardener. And through his company, we were exposed to Black and immigrant people . . . Irish, German, Italian, Jamaican, all with different accents, manners, skills, and ways. Nearly from the start, we resided in a mini-United Nations, and this gave us ease with people unlike us—people who, in many respects, often felt like family, live characters stepping from the pages of the *Geographic,* proof that our United States really was the world's melting pot. (From the first time I heard that, I've beamed with a pride that's never left me.)

We were four kids under the age of seven. My parents found a young Black woman to live with us and help manage the chaos. Overnight, she became integral to our lives: an older sister, sitter, sometimes stern taskmaster, but always clever and funny.

Typical of the times, we were taught to respect everyone, listen attentively, say please and thank you, come when called, sit still, and stop fidgeting in church. We went to school, played football in the backyard and basketball in the driveway, swam and fished and ice-skated when ponds froze over. TV was new to the world, and like most, we had favorite shows. Grandparents took us for ice cream, and sometimes to football games. We laughed, joked, wrestled, played hockey on roller skates, built boats, and made fun of one other. Boys are like that.

From an early age, I wanted to work (there's that independent streak), and began my first summer job at fourteen. I'd continue that through college. While still in high school, I worked after school and Saturdays between fall and spring sports seasons. Beginning at sixteen, I worked on construction jobs—my first tools a shovel, broom, and wheelbarrow. These led to a five-summer stint as a carpenter's helper on a crew with a pair of Ukrainians. They were tough, hard-working, sometimes intolerant overseers—but funny! After being pressed into Stalin's army, they fought on the war's eastern European front before ending their war in a German POW camp.

Within a week of my start, the foreman moved our second helper to a different crew, leaving me the sole gopher/nailer/cutter/mule. I'd done the work of two, endearing myself to the company owners for as long as I wanted that job. Other crews were populated with immigrants from Italy, Germany, Switzerland, and Hungary—all with strange accents, stories, unique ways, and senses of humor, and, to a man, grateful to be a part of the American Dream. To me, they were treasures worthy of Midas himself!

High school and YMCA athletics allowed me to experience that special feeling of being part of a team. I learned how to play by rules, why harder work and more effort were key to getting on the field, how to respect opponents—and refs too.

❖ ❖ ❖

Our dad had a rare genius to tell a million jokes and stories, and he knew a handful of special poems too. For instance, these lines from Rudyard Kipling's "If" are a touchstone for me to this day:

If you can talk with crowds and keep your virtue,
Or walk with Kings—nor lose the common touch . . .

. . . and another guiding principle is the final verse of Dale Wimbrow's "The Man in the Glass":

You may fool the whole world down the pathway of years
And get pats on the back as you pass,
But your final reward will be heartaches and tears
If you've cheated the man in the glass.

But as I aged, some of Pop's jokes and stories ceased to be funny. They'd pick on certain sorts of people, were uncomfortably "off-color," or lacked fair perspective. I was adjusting my own thoughts, learning to think independently. And I was learning, as well, that running against the grain often generates discomfort and isolation.

So it was in this crucible that my belief system began to take shape. Crosby, Stills, and Nash said it well so many decades ago, "You, who are on the road, must have a code that you can live by." Indeed!

❖ ❖ ❖

I was first out of high school and so first off to college. For me, college meant a new world: independence, more different people with different ways, college mates who actually understood professors while I struggled. My fellow students' questions often baffled me; I couldn't take notes fast enough. In addition, there were guys with athletic skills I'd seldom seen and fellows with a maturity that flummoxed me. I was raw and not very well prepared. While college was often confusing, it felt special, so I watched and listened and assimilated.

An incident that would have a considerable and lasting effect on me took place during the spring of my junior year. A 28-year-old Queens, New York bartender, Kitty Genovese, was raped and murdered on her way home from work around 2:30 a.m. The murder investigation turned up some 38 people who heard her screams and pleas for help. All turned a deaf ear, deciding not to get involved. I was mortified that people refused to go to the aid of someone in trouble.

The year before my graduation, the Viet Nam war began to heat up. The Selective Service draft was still in force, and so posed a gauntlet we'd all need to navigate. I enlisted and did my time—six years' worth—in the Air Force and Army National Guard. In San Antonio basic training, I was dumped into a barracks with 79 guys and two loud and testy drill sergeants. Again, I encountered more people, places, challenges, and experiences . . . including this gem from my Air Force sergeant, "Always be nice to the janitor. You could be working for him tomorrow."

The war became more unpopular by the day. *The New York Times* published a daily list of those who wouldn't be coming home. It was always a jolt when names of friends, fraternity brothers, and teammates would appear. By the time I'd earned my discharge, I was outraged. War was stupid, evil, perpetrated by people in powerful places who risked nothing each day. It cost lives, horrific injuries, resources, sanity, futures, and nearly destroyed our nation. I learned another lesson: that war was seldom an intelligent or humane solution to disagreement.

Once free to move about, I fled to the mountains of Colorado. It offered skies so blue as to seem painted on a gigantic canvas; mountains and rivers; new scenes, cultures, skills, sports, and people; and a marriage—all tonic to my boundless curiosity.

And then history inflicted a series of troubling incidents. The first came when Richard Nixon, the 37th president of the United States of America, having been caught lying and cheating, famously pronounced, "I am not a crook!" Yet he surely was, as the Watergate investigation proved . . . and so was forced to resign in 1974. Who'd have believed that a president would resign?

In the mid-seventies, Americans by the tens of millions viewed the television miniseries *The Holocaust* and *Roots.* I watched with both fascination and horror. How could humans treat their fellow humans with such cruelty? The stories and history seared themselves deep into my soul. The ability to hate with commitment and passion was beyond my imagination.

Finally, in the 1980s, President Ronald Reagan would ignite my passion for environmental activism when he followed the lead of his less-than-honest secretary of the interior, proclaiming that "acid rain" was but a figment of some moron's imagination. "How odd," I thought. Year after year, I'd visit high lakes on horseback. Lakes downwind of coal-burning power plants—whose only water source was rain and snowmelt—became increasingly devoid of fish. Where else would acid have come from if not from the sky? Reagan had lied to the world and those who'd put him in the White House.

After fifteen years in the mountains, I motored down the hill to Denver, a much bigger place, not so easy on the eye, but a good move to a larger community. I became a Big Brother to twelve-year old Tony, a somber and painfully shy Black youngster. We'd be together for more than eight years—constantly peering into the other's quite different worlds. A yearlong Denver leadership program opened my mind to dozens of tough issues and challenges that municipalities face the world over. It was another chunk of valuable education.

By 1987, Denver and most of Colorado were mired in another economic downturn. Remarried and with an eleven year-old son, I was offered a chance to move to North Carolina. We visited, liked what we saw—more mountains, though not so big; beaches we could reach by car; and the opportunity to be on the East Coast near my parents for the first time in twenty years.

North Carolina was culture shock in spades! It seemed we'd moved across seven international boundaries. People spoke a different language, ate different food, and used different medications, like powders to salve a headache instead of an aspirin tablet. Cars raced through the streets as though practicing for Saturday night's demolition derby.

I started a new job with a new company and became a board member of a nonprofit that served kids in distress. My son joined a Scout troop, and we explored everywhere.

After my North Carolina move, I began to sense a change in conversations with colleagues, friends, and family. Or was it a change in me? My views on issues were becoming broader and more nuanced, while theirs seemed to stay static. I'd become more perceptive—sometimes more forgiving, other times less tolerant. I felt I could see deeper, could examine with a wider perspective while others appeared immune to what Martin Luther King Jr. called "things that matter."

In the late nineties, *Sierra Magazine* handicapped possible GOP presidential primary candidates for the upcoming 2000 election. Based on his environmental record as governor of Texas, the editors concluded that George W. Bush was the very worst of the lot. Once in the White House, he proved them clairvoyant, taking a wrecking ball to as many environmental laws and norms as were within his reach. Visiting Charlotte for a fund-raising luncheon, he announced to the delight of his base that more arsenic would soon be allowed in our drinking water. Huh? For the first time in my life, I participated in a protest that day. Not long afterward, 9/11, Al-Qaeda's terroristic attacks on the

World Trade Center and the Pentagon that left almost 3,000 dead, crashed down on the U.S., and Bush led us into disastrous wars in Afghanistan and Iraq.

A half-dozen years later, I stood before that president—aloft in the balcony of a town hall meeting, microphone in hand—and said I hoped from time to time he would find the grace and humility to be ashamed of what he'd wrought. The room was packed with media, and my confrontation with the world's most powerful person went what we now call *viral.* To the world, a common man had confronted Goliath. I drew my courage from Martin Luther King, Vaclav Havel, South Carolina's *Friendship Nine,* and Elie Wiesel. Ever since, I've borne witness to the immense power of a single passionate voice when used at opportune times and circumstances. More than fifteen years later, people still tell me they've borrowed my courage of that day.

By the early 2000s, I began to notice similarities between our present-day United States and Hitler's Germany of the early 1930s. I felt an ominous foreboding as I witnessed school shootings, intolerance for immigrants, stubborn racial challenges, white supremacy, and the January 6, 2021 coup attempt on our capital. All the while, individuals at the highest levels of elected government looked away and pretended none of this was happening. Documentary filmmaker Ken Burns, however, did not look away; in 2022, he released *The Holocaust and the United States,* which depicts those eerily similar trends I've noticed.

❖ ❖ ❖

So . . . what happened to the youngster with his nose buried in *National Geographic* a lifetime ago? We've followed passages of his journey. Where is he now?

He's a passionate advocate for authentic democracy—where those elected to public office actually represent *all* their constituents. He's an environmental advocate, a voice for those less fortunate, a foil against the crazies, and recently recognized as a "whistle-blower."

He knows that all life is precious, that every one of us counts. All bring their own special gifts and stories to the table. Our differences give texture to America and make it a fascinating place in which to live our lives.

He believes in hope, hard work, ironclad honesty, persistence, vision, integrity, passion, and respect—and courage, too. He believes in truth. During a speech honoring the 100th anniversary of Nelson Mandela's birth, Barack Obama said, "You have to believe in facts. Without facts, there is no basis for cooperation. If I say this is a podium and you say it's an elephant, it's going to be hard for us to cooperate." Yeah, if we're to help our land reach its vast potential, we'll not get far without cooperation.

He believes that *who we are* is more important that *what we have.* And it's his take that we'd all do well to cherish joy and wonder and laughter.

And yet, when I peer out my window at today's America, I too often see little that comports with those beliefs. Instead, our precious democracy is under savage and relentless attack. Growing up, we were constantly told, "The Russians are coming!" But today, it's not the Russians, nor is it some other foreign power. Instead, it is citizens among us—blinded by ignorance of their own making, propaganda, greed, hate, and violence—willing to pull apart a country for the wealth, power, and ego of a few.

Democracy is where we all get to play a role in the systems that govern our lives. Why would we destroy that for which so many have sacrificed so much? Why promote the chaos, the hate, the greed? Why work so hard to prohibit others from realizing the American Dream? Why push with such enthusiasm to outlaw books and the teaching of our own history? Why malign science?

We're better than this! There is enough for all . . . if we'll care about the lives of others, about tomorrow, about peace, about sensibility. There is enough for all . . . if we'll work to be the best we can be and thus reach our full potential as a country and a world.

So it is that I write, speak, march, sing, donate hard-earned dollars. And I dream. I dream that we'll awaken and figure this out before it's too late. I believe our country, our democracy, our melting pot can survive, but not until a whole lot more of us begin writing, speaking, marching, and singing.

After all these years, I refuse to give up on our democracy. And I still hope to leave Planet Earth better than when I arrived.

So let me close with a nod to the old man in "The Bridge Builder," a poem that has been a guiding beacon for me ever since I discovered it. That man's spirit lives deep within my soul:

An old man traveling a lone highway,
Came, at the evening, cold and grey,
To a chasm vast and deep and wide,
Through which was flowing a sullen tide.
The old man crossed in the twilight dim;
The sullen stream had no fears for him.
But he turned, when safe on the other side,
And built a bridge to span the tide.

"Old man," said a fellow pilgrim, near,
"You are wasting your strength with building here;
Your journey will end with the ending day,
You never again will pass this way.
You've crossed the chasm, deep and wide,
Why build this bridge at evening tide?"

The builder lifted his old grey head.
"Good friend, on the path I have come," he said,
"There followed after me today,
A youth whose feet must pass this way.
The stream that has been as naught to me
To that fair-haired boy, may a pitfall be;
He, too, must cross in the twilight dim;
Good friend, I am building this bridge for him."

Gabriele Amersbach

According to family lore, Gabriele Amersbach and her parents came to this country with the Beatles in 1964. "I Want to Hold Your Hand" was the soundtrack to a new life. Although she learned English at age eight, writing has been her lifelong passion and her career. Armed with a master's degree in literature, she entered her professional life as a writer and communication specialist in both university and corporate settings, with a focus on health and science topics. In the last ten years, she has worked as a freelance writer and enjoys the opportunity to write about topics close to her heart. Gabriele regularly contributes articles to 50 Plus Life *magazine, which profiles older individuals who continue to contribute and enrich their world. In 2020 she began to write novels when the Covid quarantine required a mental journey to a different reality. Her personal spiritual journey includes a certification in Feng Shui that recognizes the spirit, or* chi, *in our physical environment. She volunteers at a local homeless shelter and is heartened by the goodness of people who choose hope and actively contribute to a better world.*

Welcome to My Heaven

My Evangelical Christian friend was describing a male companion she had recently met. I asked about the evening they had shared, and she told me, "Well, we are both Christians." The implication was clear: "We're in the same club—you're not." The assumptions about my own faith exasperated me. I do have a personal faith that sustains me, although it does not fit into the narrow confines of her rigid Christian beliefs. Because I have not chosen to discuss the details of my own spiritual path, she has jumped to the conclusion that I am not a believer.

My discomfort with the rigidity of so many mainstream belief systems has been the constant theme in my life. I was raised Catholic. My mother and birth father are German, and I spent the first eight years of my life in Bavaria, a mostly Catholic part of Germany. While the Catholic Church and Christianity play a visible role in the cultural heritage of the area, most Germans don't talk about religion much or even attend church. Being Catholic is part of their heritage, and those affiliated with a local church pay their annual church taxes. With that, their duty as Catholics is done. My mother was the exception in that she actually attended church and was a staunch Catholic her whole life.

When I was 7, my mother married a second time, to an American soldier (the man I considered my "Dad") who was stationed locally. After the wedding, the three of us moved to Fort Bragg, North Carolina. During the two years at the Army post, I was busy learning English and adjusting to a totally foreign culture—religion didn't take up much of my time.

That changed after Dad got out of the service. We moved to Lancaster County, Pennsylvania, a rural area in the south central part of the state. Dad had grown up here and wanted to come back home. In the heart of Pennsylvania Dutch country, the county is Bible Belt conservative. The Amish, Mennonites, and Brethren, all extremely conservative sects, had first settled this area. In the

1960s, when we moved back, the grip of rural fundamentalism was still strong. As I entered fifth grade at the local elementary school, I was regularly met with children who told me quite sincerely that I would burn in Hell as a Catholic. These conversations always ended with "You're not really a Christian."

I told my mother, of course. A busy homemaker with four young children, she would just roll her eyes as she made dinner and tell me, "Just ignore them." I got the distinct impression she thought that people who didn't consider Catholics Christians were just plain nuts and didn't deserve her attention. Armed with my mother's casual dismissal of their beliefs, I also rolled my eyes at my judgmental young friends and answered, with a laugh, "That's ridiculous," and walked away.

Yet our family couldn't get away from the impact of fundamentalism since it permeated every aspect of our lives. The small Catholic church we attended had problems finding a new location when the parish decided to build a bigger church. The plot of land that was ideal was situated next to a Church of God, whose members made it clear they didn't want a Catholic church as their neighbor. Our church found another location.

My dad's sister was especially devout and even had a gospel group that toured the country. During our family get-togethers, my cousins pressed a constant stream of leaflets into my hand. I remember two vividly: one warned of the evils of rock and roll and the other of the evils of Charles Darwin. The first leaflet told me that Simon and Garfunkel, the Beatles, and the Stones (of course) were all Satan-inspired. The second leaflet had a crudely drawn monkey on the front with a headline that asked, "Are You Really a Monkey's Uncle?" I told my mother, and we both rolled our eyes.

My aunt's family belonged to a Pentecostal church we used to call a Holy Roller congregation. We understood that members were so moved by the Holy Spirit they would shake, dance, testify, and even roll down the aisles in religious frenzy. I was never allowed to attend a service because my mother, raised on the strict standardized prayers of the Catholic Church, found these behaviors shameful and embarrassing. While I liked my aunt and her family, I spent many a childhood hour imagining the whole family rolling down the aisle of the church.

Our immediate neighbors, a pastor and his family, also made it clear that we were definitely not going to heaven. My mother, always hospitable and friendly, went out of her way to be cordial to our neighbors. She invited the adults to coffee, the children played with us daily, and she made Christmas cookies for all our neighbors. One day, the pastor's daughter, who had been playing with my sister, told her in a loud, clear voice, "My Mommy says you're not Christians." My mother was outraged. She felt that all her hospitality was being thrown back in her face. I felt even more negative about the Christian fundamentalists around us who seemed to gleefully condemn their Catholic neighbors to Hell while they munched on Mom's cake.

A few years later, we moved to another Lancaster County town that was closer to Dad's work. Our neighbors were the same—mostly very conservative church women who were quite reserved and socialized strictly with their "church family." However, my mother, undaunted, was the first woman in the neighborhood to invite the ladies over for coffee and cake on a regular basis. They came. Mom was a great cook.

At the dinner table, after hosting another neighborhood coffee klatch, my astonished mother revealed a totally unexpected side of conservative fundamentalism. These "plain" ladies wore modest head coverings, no make-up, and dowdy homemade dresses. Their churches banned drinking, smoking, card playing, and most cultural activities, including museums, the theater, and even movies. The only discussion topics left, according to my mother, were church and sex—the sex often discussed in such graphic detail that my mother was shocked. That morning she would have preferred discussing the Olympics; of course, none of the ladies had watched.

As a teenager listening to my mother's astounding revelations about our neighbors, I was struck by the hypocrisy of religions that decried so much of modern culture, especially any aspect of sex, but left women with such a limited scope of acceptable activities that sex dominated their private worlds. At the same time, I was beginning to become more aware of the hypocrisy in my own Catholic faith.

Since I didn't attend Catholic school, and my mother's interpretation of the Catholic faith was lax, I felt no personal anger about the Catholic Church's teachings. I hadn't been punished by cruel nuns or abused by priests. Church was firmly in the background of my life—except when I was confronted by righteous fundamentalists. However, I never did believe some fundamental Catholic doctrines. I knew in my heart that people of other faiths would not somehow end in limbo or worse because they weren't Catholic. Even as a child, I found this teaching too preposterous to accept. I also never believed telling a priest my sins would make them magically go away, nor did I have sins I considered particularly serious. The whole process of confession just seemed kind of weird and embarrassing to me.

Even the meat prohibition on Fridays didn't make sense. I just couldn't believe eating meat on that day was a sin—at least not until I became a vegetarian later in life and learned about factory farming. And I just didn't understand why divorced people couldn't be real Catholics anymore. In my own family, I found the whole issue riddled with hypocrisy. My mother was permitted to partake in the sacraments as a legitimate Catholic despite her divorce because her marriage to her first husband, my birth father, was officiated by a Justice of the Peace. Therefore, the marriage didn't really "count" in the eyes of the Catholic Church, and Mom could continue being a Catholic. I often thought about the impact on my mother's life if her first marriage had been in a Catholic Church. She would have been forever banned from receiving Holy Communion and the other sacraments she cherished because of her divorce, a devastating consequence.

But most of all, I resented the fact that women couldn't be priests.

This archaic rule went against every belief in the equality of women that I had nourished since early childhood. I had been taught that I could do anything, that I was smart, and that nothing could stop me if I worked hard enough. That a church believed that somehow men were superior and closer to God because of their sex and could therefore be priests, while women were relegated to "support" positions, offended me to my core. I resented that Mary, the Mother of God, had no place in the Holy Trinity. Even the Holy Spirit, a vague insubstantial figure that I never really understood, was of more importance than the mother of Jesus. That women were considered inferior ultimately eroded my commitment to Catholicism. By my early 20s, I no longer considered myself Catholic.

For the next 20 years, I was on a search to find a belief system that did not put men on top of the spiritual hierarchy. I connected the fact that an entire sex was ignored and omitted from the power structures of most world religions to the rigid laws I found so unpalatable. I believed that if religions incorporated female leaders in equal positions and honored the feminine aspect of God, not just the masculine, there would be less rigidity and more inclusiveness in all religions.

In college, I voraciously read histories that exposed the misogyny that had shaped the development of so many world religions. A deeper dive into scholarship about the origins of Christianity had me seething. According to some scholars, women *did* perform as priests in the early Christian church. As Christianity solidified as an institution that met in public arenas outside the home, men took over the leadership of the church and stripped women of all authority within it. I was outraged to read about the deliberate vilification of powerful women in the early church, like Mary Magdalen, a well-loved disciple of Jesus and a leading figure in the community around Jesus. When his male disciples abandoned Jesus during his arrest, Mary of Magdala stayed with him even through the Crucifixion. Yet later church leaders maligned her as a prostitute to diminish her powerful role in Jesus's life.

I found so many supposedly divinely inspired doctrines were actually shaped by the early misogynistic beliefs of men who were church leaders. Even Thomas Aquinas, the Italian Dominican friar and priest revered as the greatest of the medieval philosopher-theologians, sums up that women are "*deficiens et occasionatus*"—defective and misbegotten.

Eventually, I realized my anger would not right ancient—and current—wrongs. The feminine aspect of God had been severely diminished, often demonized, and ultimately repressed in most traditional religions. I could not change history. Instead, I looked for God outside of church on Sunday. Deep in my heart, I found I did believe there was a caring God who exists in some unclear form, listens to us, responds to prayer, and loves us. I felt God's presence in a moment of awe in the middle of an ancient forest, in an act of kindness that left me feeling uplifted and joyous, and in the deep love I felt for family, friends, and sometimes strangers. I started believing God was not only out there, but in each human being. We all have a choice about allowing our inner God light to shine with love, kindness, and forgiveness—or repressing the God in our nature.

After college, I eagerly explored the New Age philosophies that focused on a more personal relationship with God. In the early 1980s, my circle of friends and I started attending regular meetings with a local channeler that we found amazingly insightful and relevant. I explored Transcendental Meditation. Many of my friends explored Native American spiritualism, although it did not resonate with me. The heat of a sweat lodge was not my path to illumination.

I even explored Zoroastrianism, one of the world's oldest organized faiths, because I was drawn to the central belief that everything God creates is pure and should be treated with love and respect. The religion proscribes pollution of the rivers, land, and air. However, as I delved further, I found the religion had its own list of saints and rigid dogma. I began to understand that most world religions are similar. The differences are mostly in language, ethnicity, and cultural expression.

By my 40s, I had stopped looking for a church because none had the flexibility I longed for. However, when I adopted my daughter (age 10) at age 45, I felt the need for a spiritual community that reinforced my personal values. Living in Boston, I was intrigued by a local Buddhist community led by a kind, soft-spoken nun. I liked the focus on meditation and did not find the same rigidly prescribed doctrines that I could not accept. The belief that all life, even animals and insects, should be honored resonated with me since I take even the nastiest looking spider outside to live another day.

I decided to get involved by volunteering for a major project the nun envisioned for the local Buddhist community that summer. She wanted to start the first ever city-wide outdoor celebration of Buddha's birth. Summer was a safe choice in Boston since the celebration would not be curtailed by snowstorms that can leave roads covered in several feet of snow.

With my background in public relations, I helped to write brochures, letters, and marketing documents, and supported the nun's efforts to contact all the other Buddhist temples in the city to engage them in the project. One temple was led by a Buddhist priest who became very enthusiastic about the event—to the point that he started taking over the project. I saw him run roughshod over our gentle nun, despite the months of work she had already invested.

With aggressive sexism, he and a group of male Buddhist leaders ousted her from her own project. By the time the event was held, she had been totally sidelined and had no role in the celebration. All the lofty ideas I had about the superiority of Buddhism as a religion crumbled during those months of preparation. I saw that Buddhism as an abstract religion had many beautiful beliefs, as do Christianity, Judaism, Islam, and so many others. But it is always individuals and leaders who shape and misshape how these faith principles are expressed. I was done with Buddhism.

When I moved to Raleigh, North Carolina, a few years later, I continued to look for a community that would offer spiritual support to me and my daughter. One hot summer Sunday, I walked into a Unity Church that was rocking with what sounded like Southern Black gospel music, until I noticed the words were not quite the language of traditional hymns. Then the minister led the congregation in a meditation and started prayers with "Mother, Father God." I had found my spiritual home. Unity had the flexibility and inclusion I longed for. People of any faith—or no faith—were welcome. There were no rules. The church focused on a belief in the power of prayer and love, recognized that God is in everyone and everything, and that forgiveness is essential to releasing us from pain and sorrow—uncomplicated yet life-changing.

When I moved back to Pennsylvania a few years ago, I carried that simple formula with me. I don't have to search any more. My faith is not traditional, it follows no rules, and my heaven requires no prescribed prayers or beliefs to enter. I work on forgiving those who exclude me in their heaven. They're welcome in mine.

John Langan

On his last day of public-school kindergarten, every student but John Langan was put into line and, with fanfare, taken to visit the first-grade classroom. Left alone at his seat, John concluded he was the only student in class to have failed kindergarten. Later, at home, his mother explained his exclusion from the visit: in the fall, he would be going to a Catholic school. Despite that early trauma, John succeeded in school and eventually went on to college and graduate school—supporting himself along the way by working as a truck driver, machinist, battery assembler, hospital attendant, and apple packer. In his late twenties, he found work he loved: teaching reading and writing skills to community college students, many of whom were also working their way through school. Not satisfied with the textbooks then available, John started developing materials that would teach his students important language skills in a clear and lively way. After several years, he began publishing a series of reading and writing skills texts for McGraw-Hill. These books were successful and enabled him to form his own educational publishing company, Townsend Press, which continues to this day. John lives with his wife, Judith Nadell, near Philadelphia; and in addition to his wife (and Philly sports teams), his passions include reading and turning on reluctant readers to the pleasure and power of books. Through his Townsend Foundation, he has developed the nonprofit Townsend Library—a collection of more than one hundred books, new and classic, that appeal to readers of all ages. His foundation also funds a variety of scholarships to help deserving students pursue their dreams.

What I Believe

For much of my childhood, I imagined I knew the Truth about the big questions in life. The answers were all in the *Baltimore Catechism* provided in my early grade classrooms at St. Margaret's School in Reading, Pennsylvania. An earnest student, I did as I was told and memorized all of the essential questions and answers about life:

1. Q. Who made the world?
   A. God made the world.

2. Q. Who is God?
   A. God is the Creator of heaven and earth, and of all things.

3. Q. What is man?
   A. Man is a creature composed of body and soul, and made to the image and likeness of God.

4. Q. Is this likeness in the body or in the soul?
   A. The likeness is chiefly in the soul.

5. Q. How is the soul like to God?
   A. The soul is like to God because it is a spirit that will never die, and has understanding and free will.

6. Q. Why did God make you?
   A. God made me to know Him, to love Him, and to serve Him in this world, and to be happy with Him forever in heaven.

7. Q. Of which must we take more care, our soul or our body?
   A. We must take more care of our soul than of our body.

8. Q. Why must we take more care of our soul than of our body?
   A. We must take more care of our soul than of our body because in losing our soul, we lose God and everlasting happiness.

9. Q. What must we do to save our souls?
   A. To save our souls, we must worship God by faith, hope, and charity; that is, we must believe in Him, hope in Him, and love Him with all our heart.

10. Q. How shall we know the things which we are to believe?
    A. We shall know the things which we are to believe from the Catholic Church, through which God speaks to us.

With all these Great Truths in hand, it was my pleasure to inform my cousin, who had the great misfortune to be Protestant, that he was destined for eternal damnation. No matter what kind of life he lived, the fires of hell awaited him because I had also learned that "Outside the Church there is no salvation." So frustrated and challenged was my cousin by our endless religious debates that he went on to become an ordained minister.

I prayed a lot in my early years, having been taught that prayers were a way of piling up credits that could be redeemed after death. I prayed for indulgences—gifts from God that removed some of the temporal punishment due for our sins. With indulgences, faithful Catholics might hope to suffer less in this life and to spend less time in purgatory—a place where souls go after death to atone for their sins before ascending to heaven. Thanks to indulgences and to the sacrament of confession—where one acknowledges one's sins to a priest, does penance, and receives forgiveness—I was secure in the knowledge I was heaven-bound.

And what and where was heaven? Heaven was up there somewhere, and God was an all-powerful and all-knowing man (or woman) living way above the clouds in a great white palace beyond the reach of any space probe. And one of God's apostles, Peter, was a sentry at the gate of Heaven, providing directions for newly arrived souls to go on to heaven or straight down to the eternal fires of hell or to a temporary stay in purgatory, where a purifying fire would cleanse away their sinful residues.

But all the certainties of my childhood gave way to doubts and questions as I approached my teenage years. The shy and sweet sister of one of my childhood friends was stricken with leukemia and died soon after. Why would God allow this? And I learned from another friend that our church pastor would take altar boys out to dinner with him—and after drinking heavily, he would move his hand onto the thigh of the boy unlucky enough to be seated next to him during the car ride home. Why would God permit one of His priests to behave like this? Another priest, a religion teacher, assured our class that if we went to Mass every morning for an entire month, any request we would ask of God would be granted. I earnestly did this, arising early to accompany my devout mother to 6 a.m. Mass every morning. Why, then, did the "impure thoughts" that had begun to besiege me not go away?

While I increasingly questioned my childhood faith, I was not yet prepared to reject it. After all, my parents were Catholics, and to me the fact they were good people was a powerful argument for Catholicism. They must understand something about faith that I was not yet old enough to fully appreciate. I remember the time when the neighborhood learned that a white woman and her black male partner were to move into the row home next to my parents' home. My father was a quiet but respected presence in the neighborhood, and a group of neighbors soon appeared at his door. "What can we do to stop this?" they asked, looking to him for guidance. He shook his head in disapproval and responded, in his low-key way, that nothing would be done. "We're not like that," he simply said. His deed was more eloquent than his words, but I knew what he was thinking: that the couple were just people, after all, and they had a right to live wherever they wished. The neighbors took no action, and when the couple moved in, my parents related to them in the everyday decent way they related to everyone.

Later in adolescence, I read a little book by John Dewey titled *A Common Faith*, which argued that such timeless ideals as courage, honesty, compassion, forgiveness, and kindness were to be valued for their own sake. For the first time, it fully struck me that my parents were good people not because they were Catholics but *because they were good people*. There was no need to give the Catholic church the credit for the decent people that they were. I remember vividly the moment when I realized my parents were acting not for a heavenly reward but for the sake of goodness itself. I was sitting on a rocking chair in my bedroom, and as I continued to rock, I felt my childhood faith in Catholicism fall away. And for the first time in my life, I no longer feared in any respect the devil about whom the nuns in my childhood had told me horrific stories. With the exception of a few moments in the throes of one Stephen King book or another, that devil has never returned. I sat there and rocked on that chair and felt exhilarated and independent and free. I felt, more than ever, that the responsibility for my life and my conduct was up to me.

Another book I read soon after had an equally powerful impact on me. In his memoir *The Education of Henry Adams,* Adams described watching his beloved sister die of lockjaw after weeks of terrible suffering:

> He found his sister, a woman of forty, . . . lying in bed in consequence of a miserable cab-accident that had bruised her foot. Hour by hour the muscles grew rigid, while the mind remained bright, until after ten days of fiendish torture she died in convulsions. . . . the idea that any personal deity could find pleasure or profit in torturing a poor woman, by accident, with a fiendish cruelty known to man only in perverted and

> insane temperaments, could not be held for a moment. For pure blasphemy, it made pure atheism a comfort. God might be, as the Church said, a Substance, but He could not be a Person.

For years, I simply stopped believing in any kind of higher power. Given the countless wars and bloodshed in the world, and the endless suffering of the innocent, faith in a loving Providence and a personal God was not possible. But my view gradually became more complex as I came to appreciate that the very essence of us, our humanity, can be realized only in a world where there is no protection from suffering and death. There is a scene in Chaim Potok's *My Name Is Asher Lev* in which a boy and his father come upon a dead bird, lying on its side in the curb. The boy asks his father why the bird has died, and the father explains that everything that lives must die. Why, the boy asks, and the father replies that this is the way God made the world—so that life would be precious. "Something that is yours forever is never precious," the father says.

I realized that if I were an all-wise and all-knowing God setting the world into motion, then evil and suffering and death must hold sway for our human souls to grow and for our behavior to count. And if I were God, I could not intervene and play favorites; I would have to remain silent so men and women would be able to discover the deepest parts of themselves. At the same time, I would not allow men and women to be alone; and in the midst of the terrible challenges they would face, their souls would realize, "I am with you." In the words of Aeschylus, "He who learns must suffer, and, even in our sleep, pain that cannot forget falls drop by drop upon the heart, and in our own despair, against our will, comes wisdom to us by the awful grace of God."

At this point I decided I didn't know what to make of God after all, and I eventually found myself focusing more on the here and now. On the one hand, my belief is nicely stated in a line from W. B. Yeats: "What do we know but that we face/One another in this place?" On the other hand, I believe that the world is an infinitely mysterious place. Much of the mystery is in our conscience, the moral imperative that seems part of our human bedrock. That imperative tells us it is important to be kind to others and treat them as we would ourselves want to be treated. All the teachings of the Bible and the sacred scriptures of other religions can be reduced quite simply to "Love thy neighbor as thyself." And we don't need any of those scriptures to tell us what to do—we know it. I admired Abraham Lincoln's words about all this: "The Bible is not my book nor Christianity my profession. I could never give assent to the long, complicated statements of Christian dogma. When I do good I feel good. When I do bad I feel bad. And this is my religion."

Lincoln's words work very well for me. At the same time, on an almost daily basis, my religious instincts are engaged by the incontestable mystery and awe and wonder all around us. Let me cite just three examples:

1. A twisted young racist slaughters nine people during a Bible-study class in Charleston, South Carolina; yet the daughter of one of the victims finds it in her heart to say the following to this hate-filled man at his bond hearing:

   "I forgive you. You took something very precious away from me. I will never get to talk to her ever again. I will never be able to hold her again, but I forgive you, and have mercy on your soul. You hurt me. You hurt a lot of people. If God forgives you, I forgive you."

   Many of the other victims said similar things. Flowers piled up in front of the church where the killings took place; and in the midst of the flowers, someone placed a handwritten sign: "Darkness cannot drive out darkness; only light can do that. Hate cannot drive out hate; only love can do that."

   The amazing grace and mercy in these reactions is beyond understanding; we are left in awe and wonder at such transcendent humanity.

2. The author Alice Trillin tells a story of volunteering at a camp for children with disabilities. Alice was especially good friends with a little girl she called by her initial, L. L had genetic diseases that kept her from growing normally and from digesting food. She had difficulty walking. She had to be fed through a tube at night. Still, the little girl was, in the author's words, "the most optimistic, most enthusiastic, most hopeful human being I had ever encountered."

   As Alice became closer to the little girl, she grew more curious about L. What had given her such strength, such joy and optimism? What was her secret? Then one day at camp, while the children were playing a game, L asked Alice to hold her mail. On top of the pile was a note from L's mother. Alice glanced at it and saw the words that L's mother had written to her daughter. "If God had given us all the children in the world to choose from, L, we would only have chosen you."

   Just as humans are capable of transcendent forgiveness, they are capable of transcendent love; and in the presence of it, we are left with awe and wonder and a sense of the utter mystery of our lives.

3. The columnist Nicholas Kristof writes about a little Vietnamese girl whom he describes as "one of the mightiest people I've met, at 94 pounds. She has a towering presence, at a bit more than five feet tall."

   The eighth of nine children in a very poor farming family in the Mekong Delta, she shone in school, but her mother demanded—unsuccessfully—that she drop out of primary school and earn money as a live-in housemaid in distant Ho Chi Minh City. When the girl was in eighth grade, her mom burned her schoolbooks to try to force her to drop out, but she borrowed books and continued to

> excel. She persevered even when her parents again burned her books in twelfth grade, and as she graduated from high school, she prepared secretly for the college entrance examination. Her mother learned of this and lashed out, "I hope you fail the exams." Other students arrived at the exam location escorted by cheering, doting parents; she arrived alone, sobbing. Still, she aced the exam.
>
> With no money from her parents, college seemed unaffordable, but she saved every penny she could. She had long worked every vacation—sometimes in a factory job by day and in a duck soup restaurant by night. At college, she confined herself to a food budget of $3.50—per week. Malnourished, she toppled over in a dead faint three times in the middle of class.
>
> Professors and students discovered that she was starved and basically penniless—leaving her feeling humiliated. But it was a turning point because her teachers and classmates responded with kindness, sympathy, and help. She was then able to eat enough to keep from fainting in public. She shares a small room with two other young women, all sleeping on the floor next to each other. She studies until midnight, and then sets her alarm for 4 a.m. to resume studying. Her parents have now come around, partly because they see she will soon become an English teacher and the best-paid member of the extended family.

Such heroic strength is an inspiration to the human spirit. Not able to explain it, any more than I can explain the forgiveness and love in the previous examples, I experience her amazing grace, along with the kindness of those in her school, and I stand in awe of it. I am fully aware the world abounds in such stories; they convey truths of the soul and heart that are beyond the power of reason to understand.

With the evidence of such truths, many can make a leap of faith and believe in a loving God. I can't do this, but I align myself with the thoughts below:

- Dag Hammarskjold wrote, "God does not die on the day when we cease to believe in a personal deity, but we die on the day when our lives cease to be illumined by the steady radiance, renewed daily, of a wonder, the source of which is beyond all reason."

- Albert Einstein, while rejecting traditional religious beliefs, continually affirmed the presence of mystery in the universe and the need for a "humble attitude of mind towards the grandeur of reason incarnate in existence which, at its profoundest depths, is inaccessible to man."

I would describe myself as a spiritual person but without traditional religious beliefs. I am really interested in all the timeless questions: Who am I? Why am I here? Why are any of us here? What is life supposed to be all about? What does it mean to connect with other people?

Not knowing about life after death, I believe in life before death. This world, existence—it's all a mind-blowing mystery. We know in the deepest parts of our hearts that there is an infinite preciousness and fragility to life. We hear a voice within us that says we must do our best to care for one another and do our best to never stop seeking truth. We know that one day we will be dust and ashes, and at the same time we know that we are in the midst of wonder. We are, as Shakespeare said, "such stuff as dreams are made of."

Sally Friedman

When Sally Friedman was 25 years old, she sold her first story: the tale of giving birth to her daughter while her husband served as an impromptu obstetrician. Payment was either $12 or $12 worth of diapers. Sally chose the diapers. In the nearly six decades since then, Sally has had an illustrious career writing heartwarming, funny, and sometimes tear-inducing stories about both her family and everyday people whom she has always been "honored and privileged" to meet. Working as a journalist, Sally discovered how amazing people are, and she felt an obligation to make every person she interviewed feel important. Interviewing Holocaust survivors was some of the hardest and most important work of Sally's long career. "I have never forgotten any of them," Sally commented in an interview. "Because once you do this work, it is impossible to ever leave it behind."

What I Believe

The first glimmer I had that something awful was happening in the world was when I'd heard one of my parents say to the other, "Shhh—the *kinder!*"

Kinder is Yiddish for "children," and that's what my sister and I were during the dark days of World War II. But children are, of course, instinctive. Ruthie and I knew, without truly knowing, that what was troubling our mom and dad was something too terrible for our young ears to hear. Those hushed warnings were actually my unofficial introduction to the Nazi Holocaust. "Why are you whispering?" we would demand of our parents. But they never answered us.

My next glimmer came when people who talked strangely and had sad eyes moved into our largely Jewish Philadelphia neighborhood. On some Jewish holidays, my mother would make an extra batch of cookies or a honey cake for these people. One day, when the weather was warm, I saw that the lady getting the treats had strange marks on her arm.

"What's that?" I asked her with the total innocence of a child. It looked like paint to me.

That neighbor looked stricken, and so did my mother, who basically told me that I must never again ask about that. It would be a few years later, when I was enrolled in Sunday school at our neighborhood synagogue, that I heard about what had happened to Jews because of a man named Hitler. I learned it not so much from our teachers, but from the older kids. They loved scaring us with talk of burning people in ovens.

I begged my sister to let me sleep in her room because for a long spell, I was sure that Hitler would come after us. We were, after all, Jewish. No, ignorance was not bliss, and learning the truth wasn't much better. If there was a God, as I was learning in Sunday school, then why did that God let this happen? And if Jews were the Chosen People, what were we chosen for? Extermination? I can only imagine how many other Jewish children growing up during and after World War II struggled with that conundrum. I surely did. "Are you really there, God?" I used to ask in the dark of night.

Fast-forward a few more years, when I had let go of my image of God as a kindly and benevolent man on a throne watching over us. I had started reading, learning, listening, and sorting out my own beliefs. I was, in short, turned off to Judaism. Had there ever been a more extraordinary reason not to believe in a merciful God than the death of six million Jews, including children? I quit Hebrew school, which did not make my parents happy. But I was intransigent.

In college, I deliberately took whatever European history courses I could. Never mind that I was an English literature major. I still wanted an academic look at that chapter of history that still left me so angry and, yes, horrified. I went to synagogue with my parents on the High Holy Days because it would have broken their hearts if I hadn't. I listened to sermons about these Days of Awe when our fates would be sealed. And I thought of those gas chambers, and how horrifically so many fates *were* sealed in them.

I was married in a synagogue, again mainly because it was what was expected of me. My own personal faith was based on an ethical system I'd created for myself. I had babies of my own—three daughters—and because of tradition and expectation, I sent them off to Sunday School. They drew and colored pictures of Jewish symbols in those first years. They learned about Passover and ate matzo, the "bread of affliction," and then they chose to have Bat Mitzvahs, Judaism's welcome to Jewish obligation and commitment.

I never tried to discourage them from embracing their Judaism, but I admit it—I was relieved when they each read *The Diary of Anne Frank*. I wanted them to know all they should about this heritage, including its trail of tears and pain. It is part of who they are as Jews.

And just when I thought I'd resolved my own beliefs—still tinged with anger and disappointment at modern Jewish history—I saw a notice that would unalterably alter my faith life. It was an easy-to-miss appeal, back in the late 1980s, for people willing to participate in Steven Spielberg's crusade to try to collect the testimonies of every Holocaust survivor on Planet Earth. Steven Spielberg does not think small. To conduct the interviews with Holocaust survivors, writers were especially welcome, although that was by no means a requirement. And I had become a freelance writer who knew the ins and outs of conducting even difficult interviews. Or so I thought.

I didn't even pause to consider the complications of taking several days of training in New York City. I think I deeply, yearningly wanted to stop burying my head in the sand of anger and, instead, *do* something. Little did I know how life-altering that "something" would turn out to be. My confidence about being prepared was torn to shreds during that intensive training. Any arrogance I had about the interview process vanished.

And that humility was sobering—and so instructive. The mock interviews, the videotaping, the important history lessons, and the preparation for the varied emotional reactions we might encounter, all left my head spinning. It also left me deeply grateful that this was such a carefully constructed mission. Tampering with the scar tissue of Holocaust survivors was nothing to be taken lightly. I was awed by the responsibility. I would also learn that once you enter that secret chamber of a Holocaust survivor's memories, you can't really ever leave it behind you.

I have sat opposite men and women with stories so horrific that it was almost impossible not to gasp. As the videotape recorded their descriptions of what they had experienced—as I needed to let respectful silence sometimes reign—I also learned that in silence, some of the most important memories emerge. Not only is it golden; when we let it, silence can lead us straight back to the muffled footsteps of the soul.

It was another powerful lesson that I've never forgotten.

Nor will I ever forget the elderly rabbi whose testimony I took on a day when rain splashed down on the windows of his daughter's beautiful suburban home. The rabbi was dressed in what was probably his best suit, one a bit shiny with wear, as he recited the details of his experience, and of the losses: parents, siblings, aunts, uncles, cousins. . . . He could recite all that with remarkable calm. But when he tried to explain how it felt when a kind priest in a small French village had taken him in, had brought him a steaming cup of soup and had fed it to him because he was too weak to handle a spoon, that's when the rabbi could not go on. That simple act of kindness had left him speechless and overcome.

And yes, this rabbi had *forgiven* those who were responsible for his profound losses. It would be a pattern repeated again and again in these unforgettable interviews.

There was the lovely woman I met at her modest apartment near the University of Pennsylvania in Philadelphia, where she had become a distinguished professor. She had made tea for us and was apologetic about her chipped saucers. Those chipped saucers didn't bother me one bit, especially after I heard her story. The only child of older parents in a small town in Czechoslovakia, she had been so cherished that their only mission was to save her—not necessarily themselves. One night when she was about ten years old, they had told her to pack her warmest clothes and bundle them into a blanket. They didn't tell her why. Then they walked her into the woods not far from their home, and when they reached the densest part, they pinned a note on her coat. It simply said, "Please take care of our child."

And then these parents, who so loved their little girl, turned and walked away. They didn't stop to hug or kiss her, she later realized, in order to make it easier for her.

"Take me with you!" she begged, but they would not turn around.

She survived and lived to tell me her story because a brave and kind Christian family had found her and had taken her in. And yes, she too refused to hang onto rage. "We can't change the past," she told me quietly.

I never forgot it.

I continued to actively seek out Holocaust survivors after the formal Spielberg project had ended. I felt compelled, in my writing life, to tell their stories, and, I admit, to fathom forgiveness and faith of a kind I could never have imagined. That was how I came to interview Charlotte, a survivor who lived just a few miles from me, in a continuing care community. Our life stories could not have been more distant or different. My quiet, safe suburban life was in such stark contrast to her history, yet here we were—neighbors, both Jewish.

Her story was stark and chilling.

She and her four sisters had lived ordinary lives until Hitler changed their world in Czechoslovakia, first with the yellow stars they were forced to wear as Jewish identification, and then by being jammed into a ghetto attic. Conditions were horrendous, and food was so scarce that much of the time, they were starving. From that attic, the family members, including Charlotte's parents, were herded onto the cattle cars headed for Auschwitz Concentration Camp. So there they were, five young girls and their mother and father in a world gone mad. Their only hope in life was to stay together. To be there for one another.

That was not to be.

The girls' mother did not get past the first "selection," and died in a gas chamber at Auschwitz almost immediately after their arrival. Also in the "selection" process, Dr. Josef Mengele, well known as the Holocaust's "Angel of Death," examined each girl to be sure she was healthy enough to provide slave labor. That's when he determined that the youngest, 11-year-old Rosalie, was too thin and too weak for labor. That meant immediate extermination. And when the sisters begged and pleaded for her, Dr. Mengele offered this alternative: immediate extermination for all the sisters.

Miraculously, a mother of a child already headed for extermination volunteered to accompany her child to the gas chamber. She wanted to die with her daughter, and had seen the despair of the sisters. Little Rosalie surreptitiously changed places with that mother, and survived at Auschwitz. The miracle was that actually all five sisters survived through their wits and will. After the war, they all emigrated to the United States, are all still alive, close to one another, and still embrace life's joys, not focusing on their sorrows.

Their father, despite being desperately ill, also survived a forced labor camp, and emigrated to the United States at the end of the war. He later married a former neighbor whose own husband and two sons had been killed in the camps. He passed away about 20 years ago, having remained an observant Jew all of his life. Even after profound loss and displacement, the sisters lived full lives, had families of their own, cherished their adopted country, and still celebrate the miracle that, yes, they still have one another.

And throughout their lives, as Charlotte reported, they all still believe in God: "We forgave, not because our enemies deserved it, but because *we* deserved peace." Charlotte also suggested that in her life, she saw what corrosive hatred and anger can do.

That was it for me. I still remember how that accumulation of all the anger I had carried around for so long—all that insistence that I could never affirm faith when it seemed that God had deserted my people—kind of lifted. It was, I admit, strangely mystical. But the emotions surrounding faith are not necessarily logical. I never returned to a God with white hair sitting on a throne in a place called heaven, probably my earliest image. But I did mellow. I started trusting in that elusive "higher power" that somehow is out there/up there/and, yes, just there.

My anger dissipated. My insight about what strength and faith really mean came to the fore. And what has lingered for these many years is this: If Holocaust survivors embraced the power of forgiveness, so could I. And I now recognize that forgiveness is at the core of my beliefs.

I am proudly Jewish.

I am at peace.

Kate Zbella

Kate Zbella's life adventure began in a small town in central Wisconsin. Her two siblings, significantly older than she, left home when she was just a kid, which led her to experience life as an only child. She was fortunate to figure out, at an early age, how to forge relationships with "friends as family" and also how to enjoy her own company. (Unbeknownst to her at the time, those are really great skills to have in one's life toolbox!) At 18 she recognized that life in a small town was not for her and escaped to college. Her educational path began as a music major, redirected to journalism, ended up in psychology, and culminated in a master's degree in social work from the University of Wisconsin in 1982. She has worked in various mental health settings and has had a satisfying private psychotherapy practice for 30 years. Her beliefs are that good therapy is good education, great therapists are great storytellers, and there is immense value and comfort in simply walking on the path of life with clients, learning together how to navigate the potholes. Kate's non-work life is spent in the company of people who love her beyond her wildest expectations. She surrounds herself with people who love to laugh; appreciate great food and wine; have lively, smart, and entertaining conversations; and try to keep each other from plunging into the abyss of political and global pessimism. She also requires the blessed silence of being home alone, in many ways her natural habitat. Always believing she might have something to say as a writer, Kate was too undisciplined to do anything about it. An unexpected, serendipitous path led to the invitation to submit an essay for a book on the topic of faith and belief. She never knew that "Become a published author" was a bucket-list item until she learned that her essay had made the final cut for publication. And now she can check that box.

The Path to Faith

"As it was in the beginning . . ."

Baby: Caucasian. Sex: Female. Eyes: Blue. Hair: Blonde. Religion: Catholic.

This was the labeling on the package. And so, as a matter of Fact, not particularly Faith, I was Catholic. It was simply another identifier like the color of my skin, eyes, and hair. As such, there wasn't really a choice about it right from the get-go. At that tender age, I was in no position to make a choice. But lying there, securely and blissfully swaddled, in my pre-verbal infant state, little did I know that this identifier was going to be stuck like glue to me for the rest of my life, nor how much of an impact it would have on nearly every facet of my existence—my sense of self and self-esteem, my overall grounding in the world. It was an assigned part of my identity and that was simply that. I was Catholic.

In the early 1960s, growing up in a small town in central Wisconsin, in a neighborhood full of kids, there was an unspoken pecking order, strangely enough, having to do with what religion you were.

There were the Catholics—the "Superior" ones, particularly if you had the good fortune to attend the parish school and be taught by the good nuns. The second-tier Catholics were the kids who went to the public school ("the Publics") and were resigned to attending CCD (Confraternity of Christian Doctrine) classes on Saturday mornings (rendering them unable to play until after lunchtime, which threw a major wrench into the apparatus of weekend fun in the 'hood).

Then there were the Lutherans. There was a vibe, covertly encouraged by the good Catholic parents, that prompted us to think of them as "less than." They were "not like us," in that Superior Catholic (i.e. "We're going to heaven and you're not") sort of way. Somewhere along the line, maybe in about fourth grade, there was a reference to Martin Luther being a "heretic." At the time I realized it was not such a great label to have someone hang on you, but it sort of completed the circle for me about why the Lutheran kids (who were perfectly good playmates, in my opinion) were okay to hang around with, but certainly not to be selected as a "best friend" or sleep-over candidate. After all, they were "heretics." Whatever that meant.

And then there was the lone Jewish family, a mom, dad, boy, and girl. I don't recall ever hanging out with them. In fact, I don't recall ever even seeing much of them, though they lived right in the next block. In retrospect, given the neighborhood religious demographics and aforementioned pecking order, they were probably afraid of the sheer mass of us Christians or, at the very least, wanted nothing to do with us. Can you blame them?

Anyway, the '60s were an interesting time in the Catholic Church. I was raised on the Latin Mass, with hours spent in church at insufferably long services, the smell of incense (which **would** unfortunately often induce vomiting in some kid, inevitably sitting right behind me), and lots of kneeling, all the while following along in a Latin/English prayer book to facilitate understanding whatever the heck was going on. The rituals were weird and strange and, at the same time, comforting and familiar.

And then Vatican II came along, stirring up some very disorienting changes and leaving quite a ruckus in its wake. There was the exchange of the Latin Mass for a more "user-friendly" English liturgy, the altar was turned around to face the congregation instead of the wall, and the good nuns traded in their dour black habits for lively colored polyester "leisure suits." It was the beginning of a new "ecumenical" church culture that was becoming more "hip" (guitar Masses!) and more accepting of people who "weren't like us" (turns out that people other than Catholics might be able to get to heaven after all).

Anyway, this was all I knew of religion, and my parents were particularly steeped in it. They were involved in many facets of the life of our parish as volunteers, my mom helping in the kitchen for wedding and funeral dinners, attending "circle" meetings and retreats; my dad counting money on Sunday mornings with his guy friends; and the two of them working together, year after year, on the "Parish History Scrapbooks" many long nights at the kitchen table.

And so I found my niche in the operation as well. I started out helping clean the church on Saturday mornings (which was down-time for playing anyway, as half the neighborhood was in their CCD classes). But later on, around sixth grade, because I was one of those kids who got signed up for music lessons as soon as I could sit upright on a piano bench so had amassed some serious experience at the keyboard, I became a church organist. And not just any old church organist, mind you. I'm not one to boast (one of the Seven Deadly Sins, I believe), but I was really good. Truth be told, I could lead a congregation in song like nobody's business. I played the massive organ with a confident panache, a vim and vigor that the other, more seasoned, organists lacked. My secret? I snuck into church once with a Lutheran friend of mine and heard what those Lutherans did with "A Mighty Fortress Is Our God." Holy mackerel! Those heretics could sing! The organist played loud; the congregation sang loud and on pitch; it was impressive. So I covertly adopted a decidedly Lutheran way of playing the organ in our feeble-voiced Catholic congregation, and over the years people would routinely tell my parents that they knew right away who was playing the organ that day. I think they meant it as a compliment.

So all of this lead-up has been about "religion," and not really about "faith and belief," which is the topic at hand. See, as a kid, the two were one and the same for me. I was Catholic. I went to Catholic schools—grade school, high school, college. And I believed what I was taught to believe in religion class. I aped the behavior and values of my parents like a good, obedient kid. But once my formal Catholic education was winding down, I began to navigate in a world where I discovered that my rote belief system and its rules were not that easy to blindly accept anymore. It threw me for a loop.

In college I was faced with my first real dilemma of faith when a close friend had gotten pregnant and chose to have an abortion. It was a Catholic college. She grew up Catholic, the same as me. And she swore me to secrecy about her plan. Back in those days, abortion was rarely talked about. What I did know about it was that it was, supposedly, killing a baby, and therefore very wrong. So being young and naïve in the ways of the real world beyond Catholicism, I decided I needed to talk about it. I broke her confidence and shared the information with a mutual friend of ours, who proceeded to confront her and try to talk her into having the baby. Not only did that not work, but my friend was horrified at my betrayal, and all of us felt really bad about it for a really long time. So, as it turns out, real life and faith and belief and religion don't always get along, do they?

By the time I was in my late 20s, I was more and more disgusted with Catholicism. The notion of old white men wearing ermine capes and Prada loafers in Rome telling poor women in overpopulated Third World countries that they were not to use birth control, and certainly not ever consider abortion, appalled me. The realization that the Vatican had amassed multi-trillions of dollars' worth of property and artifacts, which appeared to be valued more than helping solve world poverty and other things that I'll bet Jesus might have preferred, was beyond hypocritical. The person I was evolving into, the way I ended up living my life, did not reflect the recipe of formulaic Catholicism I was raised with. I became disenfranchised. "Fallen away," they termed it.

But here's where my "path to faith" really begins. I possessed the historical foundation of Catholicism, and I acquired the intellectual and philosophical exposure to other belief systems from atheism to paganism to evangelical fundamentalism. But most of all, I had the visceral knowledge and lived experience of watching my mother and how she lived her faith. For as long as I can remember, as a kid sitting next to my mom in church, and later in life as a dutiful adult daughter attending church with her (out of respect for her, not out of my own inclination to be there), I remember her being brought to tears when she prayed. Whether it was at Mass, or at home in her chair reading her stack of holy cards and prayers, she would always tear up. As a kid I found it curious;

as an adolescent I found it embarrassing. But now, as an adult, I get it. When my mother prayed, she brought all of her burdens and worries and joys to the experience. Her private conversation with Jesus, Mary, or whichever saint she was chatting with at the time, was intimate. These relationships were possibly the most intimate of her life.

My mother was the embodiment of a good Catholic woman and mother. She was feisty and durable, but she could be a pistol, too. She told me, not so many years ago, that I would be going to hell for some of the life decisions I'd made. I reminded her that I didn't really think that was her call, but it was a pretty hurtful thing to say to a kid who (she also felt) was "doing so much to help other people." But in her later years, she mellowed; and over time it became evident to me that all of those years of unwavering, persistent devotion to her faith and her daily prayers had been her lifeline to gratitude, joy, and at times, her sanity. This was especially true after the unexpected death of my dad just two months after I left home to go to college. Suddenly a widow in her mid-50s, her beloved, kind, funny husband ripped away from her without warning, and her youngest child having just left the nest, she was scared, sad, and unhinged. But what I witnessed then, and acutely realize now, is that she never stopped believing. Though she felt lonely and abandoned, she knew she was safe in the hands of her God as long as she kept up her part of the relationship. And that she did. My mother showed me what it looked like to believe.

"Is now . . ."

My mom died in late September of 2015, just a few weeks short of her 99th birthday. One morning in late July I got the call that all adult children with an elderly parent anxiously await, telling me that she was en route to the hospital with a serious medical incident. Intuitively I knew that this was not going to end well for her, although she was, reportedly, alert and cracking jokes with the EMTs. As it turns out, my prediction was accurate; and a few days later she was admitted to the local hospice facility—a place that, ironically, she frequently talked about since many of her friends and relatives had cycled through there and had given it rave reviews.

By any account, my mother was a very old woman. But she was remarkably healthy for her age, mentally sharp, and had a great sense of humor. So, true to her durable form, her time in hospice defied the experts' predictions of "a few days . . . maybe two weeks tops." It was clear she was not going anywhere until she was good and ready and, though weak and tired, she played out the better part of seven weeks preparing herself to die, all the while keeping up the most important ritual of her daily life—the saying of her favorite prayers. She would ask my sister and me to read them to her each day, morning and evening. It was a ritual I cherished, and I found it was as comforting to me as it was to her; it was one of the remaining things we could still do together.

There was one thing in life, however, that she wanted more than anything else. She repeatedly asked for it, but was never able to get it from me. As a last-ditch effort, she even went so far as to rouse herself from a deep sleep during one of her final weeks in hospice to reach for my hand, look into my eyes, and plead one more time: "I wish you would go to church." At the time, I could only sigh, kiss her cheek, and say "I know." But after she died, I realized that honoring her request became as important to me as it was to her.

Once I left my small town home at age 18 to go to college, I never returned. After graduation I settled in a big city about four hours away. My mom visited me there only infrequently, and the last time she did was at least 25 years ago. So one Sunday, she needed to go to Mass; and since I was not a practicing Catholic and, therefore, didn't belong to a church, I took her to an ancient church in the heart of the city. It was modest and unassuming on the outside, but inside it was an architectural gem. It was an old-fashioned Catholic church, filled with statues and images of all of the saints my mother loved and knew so well. Despite being a visitor, she immediately felt at home there. Over the years, she asked me many times if I'd go there and light a candle for her. I always said yes, but never quite got myself there to do it. I'd find myself lighting candles for her in other places all over the world, but not in the one church she visited and couldn't forget.

Literally on her deathbed, my mother was busy giving orders. One of them was to have a number of Masses said at this beloved church for various relatives and friends, and one for herself. I assured her I'd take care of that, and so once she was gone and the funeral was over, I contacted the church to make arrangements for the Masses and to ask if there was one available on her upcoming 99th birthday, though I realized it was short notice. I explained that she was recently deceased, and though she had been only an occasional visitor, she had a special fondness for the place. And, because there are no accidents in life (a "belief" of mine), it turned out there was in fact a Mass available to be said in her memory on her birthday, that next week. It was to be the birthday present from me that she had always wanted.

So off I went, early on that dark, chilly morning, and I sat in the back, on the side of the church with the Mary statue—the maternally preferred location throughout my long-abandoned days of church-going. And it was here that I finally began to sink into grief. When I heard the priest say my mother's name as he invoked the prayer for "those gone on to the promise of eternal life, and whom we remember in a special way today," it was all I could do to stifle the deep, wailing sobs I felt inside. (Regrettably, I had no tissues at hand, making quite the mess of things for myself.)

I even went to communion, something I had refrained from for many years. When the priest gave me the host, I replied "Thank you," only later remembering the correct response is "Amen."

And when the Mass was over, I did what she had asked me to do dozens of times. I lit a candle for her and sat at the feet of the giant ceramic Mary, the icon that was her rock and her inspiration for 99 years. And there, in the peace and the quiet, I felt the solace that she must have felt for all of those years. Then, in my head, the music started: "When I find myself in times of trouble, Mother Mary comes to me . . ." And at that moment, I felt two Mothers keeping watch over me. I realized that I could finally let go of my

Catholic cynicism and rebellious railing against her insistence that I "go to church," finally realizing that it doesn't have to mean the same thing to me as it did to her. My faith could just be about me returning to a place that felt familiar and being comforted by that. My wise mother gave me a birthday present too that day. She led me to that moment to tell me I can just "Let It Be."

"And ever shall be . . ."

In the self-help literature about adults and their adjustment to the loss of both parents ("adult orphans," we're called), copious permission is given to be at loose ends for a bit, with many caveats about how long that might take and the unanticipated things one might feel. In my work as a psychotherapist for over 30 years, I've navigated the path of grief with many of my clients in the wake of their parents' death. I've been a trusted companion walking next to them on an uncharted path toward a level of individuation that happens only when, suddenly, all of your elders are gone and you become the oldest generation in your family. So while I've had a clinical appreciation and understanding of the process, it's only now, walking that uncharted path myself, that I realize the layers of complexity at hand are far deeper than the intellect alone can navigate. And so, once again, another path to faith begins, here and now.

Hindsight being 20/20, I see that my journey of belief over 50-plus years has been a kaleidoscopic mix of thoughts, feelings, confusion and various ways of displaying my faith—or lack thereof—to the world. From my early Catholic roots, to the rejection of organized religion altogether, to the adoption of a more philosophical worldview, rich with elements (and helpful psychotherapeutic tools, by the way) of Buddhist thought and sensibility, to now—feeling a surprising and unexpected pull to return in some way to the familiar, comfortable structure of my mother's faith—I have understood my personal belief system to be an organic, living process, constantly in a state of evolution.

Among the only things I really wanted of my mom's remaining possessions were the hoards of holy cards and prayers and clippings of articles she found inspirational. The words on all of these random slips of paper possess an energy that feels like a living, breathing connection to her. They were her lifelong companions, whether to ease her mind in times of despair or express gratitude for all she had been given. And now I find they are serving as my road map: as guides for me on the next leg of this journey of belief.

Like many people, I've taken a rather circuitous route, from my pre-assigned Catholic foundation to my pursuit and acquisition of theoretical constructs; to a myriad of life experiences; to a career spent, among other things, helping people discern the difference between "religion" and "spirituality" and how their personal journeys, much like my own, have shaped their understanding of faith, and whether there is a need for it at all as one moves through life.

So, here and now, what I have come to believe is this:

- I believe the old adage is true—"The Lord works in mysterious ways." How else to explain the things in life that defy logic and reasonable explanation? The powerful synchronicities that occur, often prompting a "Wow. How'd that happen? You can't make this stuff up!" Lost objects that suddenly reappear, after decades of fruitless searches. Thinking about someone and, simultaneously, having the phone ring only to hear their voice. So whether I refer to these things as evidence of "God" or "the Universe" or "energy," I interpret these events as reminders that there is another, decidedly mysterious, force at work.

- I believe the teachings of wise elders of varying stripes, whether the Catholic Jesus or the Protestant heretics or Buddha and the Eastern mystics or a bevy of new-age philosophers, all say pretty much the same thing: Be kind; help those less fortunate than you; forgive those who hurt you; say "please" when you need help and "thank you" when that help arrives; operate in humility and gratitude always; and, most of all, never lose sight of the fact that you are not in charge. That something/someone/some energy somewhere is. And that it can't really be explained. And that's why they call it "faith."

- I believe that there is something to be said for not-knowing. That an anchor of some sort of faith or belief allows for the relief of surrender, which can be a comforting thing. When life throws us uncatchable curve balls, or an obstacle appears on our path that seems insurmountable, having a structure of faith or belief to lean on reminds us that all is exactly as it should be, all of the time—whether it appears that way or not.

It's ironic and sad, in a way, that this next leg of my journey of faith comes as a response to the death of my mom. If she were here, I'd be telling her the stories of all of the crazy things, the odd synchronicities, and the unexplainable random events that have happened since her departure. I'd tell her that I'd been to her favorite church and how I've been reading through her prayers and how they feel comforting to me now. And she'd listen intently and tear up, filled with gratitude that her long-standing prayer had finally been answered.

But I don't have to have her here to tell her all of this. She already knows. Many times when I meditate, she comes and stands next to me, leaning on her walker. Sometimes she brings a saint or two with her, as if to let me know they are listening and bringing whatever help it is I need that day.

So am I just making this up? Is this just my conscious mind creating a narrative that soothes my heart when I miss her? Perhaps. But it doesn't really matter.

Because it's evidence to me that I do, in fact, have faith. And that, no matter what lies ahead on the path, it will never be all that far away from me after all.

"World without end. Amen."